# SHALLOW GRAVES IN SIBERIA

This book is at once excellent for its style and clarity, and appalling for its content of brutality. Michael Krupa, born Polish, was accepted by a Jesuit seminary, from which he ran away, before he had taken his final vows, to join the army. He survived the German attack on Poland, only to be arrested on entering the Soviet-occupied half of his country, and packed off – via the Lubianka prison in Moscow – to a labour camp in Siberia. From this too he was able to run away, thanks to his own strength and courage, to luck, and to total strangers who supported him on the run. He now lives quietly in Yorkshire, and has written in old age an extraordinary testimony to the strength of the human spirit when it has to contend with beasts in human form. Read it and admire his strength of heart.

M.R.D. Foot

*In loving memory of my wife, Kathrene,*
*who died peacefully in her sleep, 30 March 2004*

# SHALLOW GRAVES IN SIBERIA

## Michael Krupa

BIRLINN

This edition published in Great Britain in 2004 by
Birlinn Ltd
West Newington House
10 Newington Road
Edinburgh

www.birlinn.co.uk

Reprinted 2010, 2013

First published in 1995 by Minerva Press

ISBN 978 1 84341 012 6

British Library Cataloguing-in-Publication Data
A catalogue record for this book is available
on request from the British Library

Typeset by Hewer Text Ltd, Edinburgh
Printed and bound by Grafica Veneta

www.graficaveneta.com

# Foreword

For a number of years before he retired in 1980, the University of Bradford had, as a member of its security team, a conscientious and likeable man of Polish origin known to everyone as Michael. I knew him well in my role as Pro-Chancellor of the University and now, some years later, I have come to know him differently and better through his writings.

Michael called to see me at my home to ask if I would read the book he had written in retirement about his early life and about which he spoke with much sincerity and conviction. It tells a story which is gripping in its sense of determination and it informs the reader about facts which I recall, through having served with Polish officers and troops during the Second World War in Scotland, Palestine and Italy.

I have heard many stories of escapes and of valour but this one by Michael surpasses all others. It is an enthralling account that will teach its readers a great deal. If its writer believes, as he says, that he owes this country gratitude, he showed it adequately by his work at the University. He was part of a very good team but I doubt if any of them really knew what he had undergone in his early years. I commend this story to the readers.

A.J. Thayre, CBE, Hon D. Litt, DL
Pro-Chancellor of the University of Bradford
Former Chief General Manager and
Director of the Halifax Building Society
Former Lieutenant-Colonel, the Highland Light Infantry.

January 1988

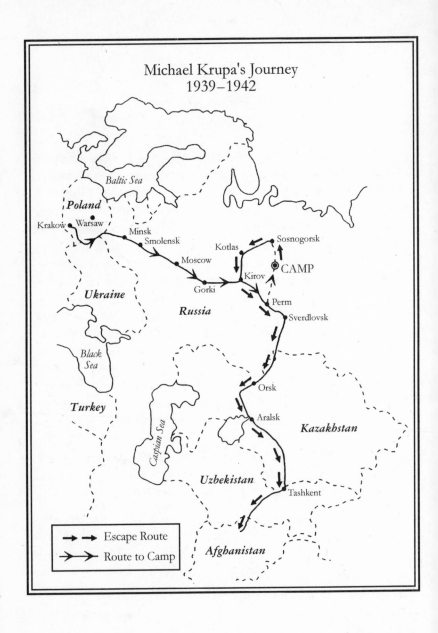

# Michael Krupa's Journey
## 1939–1942

*Baltic Sea*

**Poland**

Krakow • • Warsaw • Minsk • Smolensk • Kotlas • Sosnogorsk

*Ukraine*

Moscow

⊙ CAMP

Gorki

Kirov

*Russia*

Perm

Sverdlovsk

*Black Sea*

*Caspian Sea*

*Turkey*

Orsk

Aralsk

*Kazakhstan*

*Uzbekistan*

Tashkent

**→ →** Escape Route

**→→→** Route to Camp

*Afghanistan*

# Introduction

Modern Russia has been a nature reserve – of human nature. Michael Krupa encountered Russia in its most forbidding and isolated form, as Stalin's Soviet Union. And there, as this book records, this astonished foreigner met ancient and endangered species now rare in the West or preserved only within the realms of fiction. For example, blackguards, lickspittles, holy fools, slyboots, mountebanks, cacodemonic sadists – and also souls of crystal purity and goodness.

Michael Krupa ran across all of them during his torments as a convicted 'spy' in the labour camps and then on his perilous escape to freedom across the wartime Soviet Union. From the snowbound Pechora logging camps in the far north, he travelled by horse, train and finally on foot over the whole colossal breadth of the Soviet Union. Finally, emaciated and dizzy with joy, he dodged over the Uzbek border into Afghanistan.

During the long months of his journey, he wore several disguises: a telephone linesman, a railway ticket inspector. In the Soviet Union, a uniform radiated awe and fear and was an indispensable instrument for bluff. But in reality Michael Krupa was Polish, brought up in a village in the mountains and intended by his parents for the priesthood. Accepted as a novice by the Jesuits, he eventually rebelled against monastery discipline and went over the wall. But that first escape was soon followed by his conscription papers. He was called up into the Polish army in 1939, as the forces of Hitler and Stalin invaded his country from either flank and abolished its independence.

To understand what followed for Krupa, now and in the next few years, it helps to have a summary of the broader political events. Hitler and Stalin, deadly foes until then, had staggered the world in August 1939 by signing the Nazi-Soviet Pact of non-aggression. Unknown to the rest of the world, the Pact had secret clauses agreeing to partition and abolish Poland. Germany invaded Poland on 1 September, the Soviet Union invaded on 17 September, and the partition line between them was set along the river San. All the Polish cities and provinces east of the line were annexed by the USSR, and, the following year, the Soviet authorities began to deport their Polish civilian population. Something like half a million Poles were sent to Arctic labour camps or to central Asia, where the terrible conditions meant that the death rate among the deportees was perhaps 30 per cent each year. Meanwhile, on Stalin's direct orders, over 20,000 officer-prisoners, policemen and other officials were secretly shot (the well-known Katyn massacre was only a small part of this operation to exterminate Poland's elite).

But in June 1941 the situation suddenly changed. Hitler invaded the Soviet Union and the Poles became potential allies for Stalin. Under an agreement with the Polish government in exile in London, the Soviet authorities granted all Polish deportees an 'amnesty' (though they had committed no crime) and allowed them to leave the Gulag. Polish prisoners of war were also freed.

Those who were still alive and able to travel made their way towards camps in the southern USSR, where General Władysław Anders was setting up a free Polish army. In March 1942, with Stalin's agreement, the Anders army took ship across the Caspian Sea to Iran, and left the Soviet Union for ever. The army was accompanied by a huge number of civilian women and children, survivors from the Gulag or from the steppes of Kazakhstan. Many thousands of Poles were unable to reach the Anders army bases in time and had to be left behind. Those who did reach Iran had mostly been reduced to desperate physical condition by hunger and disease, and required months of rehabilitation. From Iran, the civilians were relocated to a variety of British colonies to await the end of the war. The soldiers (reorganised into the Polish Second Corps) moved to Iraq and Palestine for training, and eventually joined the war on the Italian front.

After 1945, a Polish state was restored, but under Communist rule and within different frontiers. The Soviet Union refused to give up the eastern Polish provinces it had seized in 1939. As the Second Corps was largely composed of solders from those border-lands, many of whom had experienced for themselves the reality of Soviet Communism, most of the officers and men decided not to return to the new Poland but preferred to live as exiles in Britain, North America or elsewhere.

This was the tragic background to Michael Krupa's story. But it's important to notice that his own fate in this fearsome historical landscape was not typical. He did not come from the eastern borderlands but from southern Poland, from regions occupied by the Germans in 1939. Secondly, he did not enter Soviet captivity as a prisoner of war or deportee. Instead, seeking his parents after the fighting was over, he deliberately crossed the San river into Soviet-held territory, having heard in his native village that his parents had fled eastwards across the demarcation line to escape the Nazis.

Here he made a catastrophic mistake, which almost cost him his life. Krupa spoke fluent German (his mother was Austrian), and had used the language to wangle a Nazi laissez-passer to help him move around the German occupation zone. Assuming, foolishly, that the Russians would welcome anyone fleeing from the Nazis, he failed to destroy this pass when he crossed the river. The result was that he was instantly arrested as a Germany spy. Unbelievably lucky not to be shot on the spot, he was transferred to the Lubianka prison in Moscow and there, beaten into signing a 'confession', he was sentenced to ten years in the Pechora Gulag complex, to be followed by life in Siberian exile.

It was this sentence which made Michael Krupa's case special. It meant that – unlike the hundreds of thousands of Polish deportees who never had the distinction of a trial – he could not qualify for the 1941 'amnesty'. He was a convicted criminal, who had confessed to a grave offence under Soviet law. It was the realisation that he had no hope of release, and that he would be lucky to survive another year of Pechora's regime of starvation, bullying and overwork, that resolved him to plan an escape.

The rest of the book is the thrilling, often touching, story of his immense journey from the Arctic to the Afghan border. And here the reader requires a warning and a reassurance. This book, Krupa's narrative, has nothing whatever to do with the well-known but largely discredited bestseller *The Long Walk*. Published first in 1956 and written ostensibly by the late Sławomir Rawicz with 'ghosting' assistance from a British journalist, *The Long Walk* purported to tell how a party of prisoners escaped from a camp in the Gulag and walked across the Gobi Desert and Tibet to British India. Although the book inspired a feature film (*The Way Back*) in 2010, inconsistencies and conflicts of evidence have knocked much of the credibility out of the original book in recent years. While one vague British report did suggest that a trio of Siberian convicts reached north-eastern India during the Second World War, it now seems highly unlikely that Rawicz was among them or anywhere near Tibet. Instead, his military record, recently un-earthed, shows that he was evacuated from the Soviet Union to Iran with the rest of the Anders army.

Krupa's story, in contrast, is about people as well as about feats of endurance. In the course of his imprisonment and then his escape, he met a sequence of extraordinary human beings, some saintly and some satanic, who impressed themselves on his memory. He is as much concerned to remember and understand them as he is to recount his own struggles to survive the snow, the starvation and the security police, and it is this unquenchable curiosity which makes *Shallow Graves in Siberia* so convincing and so compelling.

In the Pechora camps, he was confronted by the terrifying Commissar Kurylo. The prisoners were made to watch as he executed recaptured escapers by slashing them apart with the sickle of the camp's hammer-and-sickle escutcheon. And yet two years later the same Kurylo was plying Krupa with cigarettes, chocolate, vodka and sympathy in order to persuade him to work outside the camp as a telephone linesman.

Krupa used this chance to escape through the forests, losing his horse to hungry wolves, and reached a railway station where his telephonist uniform got him to the front of the food queue. There he teamed up with three criminals, also on the run, and broke into a series of goods trains which took them as far as the city of Perm. Now their luck ran out. After breaking into a sealed wagon to steal food and vodka, destined for troops at the front, they were arrested in a state of drunken stupor by a military patrol which dragged them out into the snow for immediate execution. The three thieves were killed, and Krupa was left for dead after a bullet passed through his neck.

But two devoutly religious Russian peasants, a married couple employed on the railway, saw the four bodies lying in the snow and decided out of sheer piety to bury them. When they found that Krupa was still alive, they carried him home and hid him in the hay loft, where his wounds slowly healed over many months. 'They couldn't have treated their own son with greater kindness and love,' Krupa writes. But their real son Yuri was a slave labourer in the Kolyma gold mines, condemned for failing to report a friend who had insulted the Soviet flag. Yuri had worked as a ticket inspector on the railways, and in a final gesture of sacrifice, his parents gave Michael Krupa his uniform and his railway pass.

With this priceless equipment, Krupa set out again to bluff his way southwards towards the Soviet border, still two thousand miles away. Many adventures followed, as he rode the trains and posed as a ticket inspector, and many strange encounters. Krupa came across a beautiful young woman who was also a fanatical Party member, a mob of drunken, ragged Kazakhs on their way to join the army, an officer who began to suspect that he was an imposter, a mafia of armed Arab smugglers in Tashkent who also saw through his disguise but decided to protect him and help him on his way. All are sharply observed and reported, sometimes with affection, down to the Uzbek shepherd family who helped him on his last miles towards the Afghan frontier.

Some of the few foreigners who witnessed the Soviet Union in wartime – its titanic sufferings, migrations and sacrifices – felt afterwards that they had seen a panorama of heroism on a scale which had no parallels in history. Michael Krupa saw it all rather differently. As a Catholic Pole, he could only recognise Russia and its Soviet successor as the traditional arch-enemy of his country, and the murderer of its hard-won independence. And yet in this book he also makes a very Polish distinction between Russian power and individual Russians, perceived with pity and with sympathy for their warm, underlying humanity which 'the system' in all periods has worked to suppress.

After the war, Michael Krupa learned that both his parents had died as a result of their treatment in the Soviet Gulag. He found a job in Yorkshire, married an English girl and lived at peace. Until he wrote this book, few people close to him knew how profoundly he had earned that freedom and that peace.

Neal Ascherson
March 2013

# Chapter One

## *Polish Highlander*

In south-west Poland, near the ancient Polish capital of Kraków, on the road running from Wadowice to Myslenice and then further south to the Tatra Mountains and beautiful Zakopane, lay a small Polish village called Rudnik. Its peasant population numbered no more than a thousand.

Each peasant household had a small piece of land which stretched out towards nearby Dalin, a mountain completely covered with birch, pine and fir trees. Wild mushrooms grew there in abundance, and on its lower woodland slopes during the summer months spread a carpet of bilberries, raspberries and blackberries.

In the warm mountain climate the peasants tended their gardens, nurturing their aged apple, plum and pear trees which had outlived many generations. The villagers were self-sufficient, most of them owning a few cows, hens and goats. The richer ones fattened up pigs and every family possessed a horse and a hay cart.

Although the major occupation of the peasant householders was the cultivation of their land, practically every highlander was also a born carpenter or builder. Each had built his own house on the land left him by his father. The houses were simply constructed. The foundations were large flatstones cemented together, and the walls were built from the logs of fir trees firmly fitted to one another. The insides of the walls were covered with large wooden planks, smoothly planed and then varnished. The roofs were made of straw and wooden shingles.

Accommodation was sparse. There were usually two rooms, one

1

a large living kitchen with a huge primitive stove, a big pine table well-scrubbed each day (the focal point of all household activities), and a set of wooden benches pulled up close to the stove on cold winter nights. Two or three large wooden pallets filled with straw and covered with large, soft, feather eiderdowns served as beds for the children of the family.

The second room doubled as a 'best room' during the day and a bedroom for the husband and wife at night. The wooden walls were hung with pictures of the Blessed Virgin Mary and Jesus Christ since most of the peasants were deeply religious and family prayers were said each night before the children went to bed.

The highlanders not only built their own houses but also decorated them with highland sculptures, some of which are still evident today in the ancient villages scattered at the foot of the mountains. The villagers also made their own musical instruments from the yew trees, which grew in abundance on the lower mountain slopes. Music-making and dancing were their only entertainments.

On Sundays, Polish highlanders dressed up smartly to attend church. The men wore light woollen trousers decorated with a red cord along both sides of the leg. The side pockets were embroidered with a picture of a thistle. Light leather sandals were fastened to their ankles with strong goat-skin straps. Each man wore a white flaxen shirt and a hat decorated with white beads sewn on to the brim. However, the most important part of this Sunday dress was the so-called *clupaga* which served both as an axe and a walking stick. Its shaft was made from the wood of the hazelnut tree and its head was beaten into shape from heavy metal. On weekdays peasants used it as a support when climbing the rugged mountain slopes. On Sundays and festivals, however, it was carried as an ornament in the highlanders' dance celebrations, representing their unity against their enemies.

On these days, too, peasant women also dressed in style, in colourful embroidered skirts and white embroidered blouses, with soft boots laced up to the knees and their long, thick hair held in place by a woollen travelling scarf. Every Sunday the family's horse would be washed and groomed and the cart polished. The family would then travel in it to church to pray to God for peace and prosperity.

It was in this wonderful little village that I was born over seventy years ago, to a Polish father and an Austrian mother. My father was a manager of a small agricultural shop, supplying the villagers with utility goods like paraffin, candles (there was no electricity or gas in the village), sugar, matches and cigarettes. The barter system applied to all transactions since money was scarce and sometimes non-existent. Eggs, butter, cheese and fruit would be brought to the shop and exchanged for paraffin, sugar or, if the price was right, cigarettes. Once the deals were completed, my father trundled his cart laden with fresh produce to Kraków market where he would stay until the very last egg was sold, buying fresh provisions out of the profits. Bartering would start again the following day.

In many ways this was a hard and demanding life. Nevertheless the highlanders were free to travel from village to village, from the countryside to the town, and from one country to another. They were free to go to church, to enjoy their drinking, dancing and music-making, and to speak openly of their lives and loves.

Rudnik boasted one elementary school and here I took my first steps in education. My brother Wladek was two years older than me but I caught up fast and soon we were in the same class. I was good at maths, reading and writing but not so good at obeying school rules. I was always being punished by the teachers for fighting and trouble-making. Punishment was either a smack on the hand with a ruler or detention after school.

When I was about seven, I was doing one of my frequent spells of detention in the schoolmaster's study. The door was locked and I was under instructions to finish some work. Being bored I opened the window, perched on the window sill and dropped into the schoolmaster's vegetable plot. Making sure no one had seen me, I raced off home where, needless to say, I had to suffer a good thrashing from my father. The schoolmaster was so grateful that I had not broken my neck in the escape that he refrained from detaining me for several weeks.

Looking back, I remember always being good at jumping. My brother Wladek and I used to play in the barn when father was away at the market. We would dare each other to jump out of the barn window and into the hay, a distance of about eight metres. While Wladek was always apprehensive, I would rush headlong out of the window, tumbling feet first into the soft hay, laughing and shouting all the way down. Later in my high school days I became high school champion at skiing, jumping 40 metres in the ski jump event. This fearless quality stayed with me throughout my life and is probably the reason why I am still alive to tell this story.

At high school in Sulkowice, I settled down to work. Natural history was my favourite subject. The forests, the smell of the pine woods, the streams cascading down the mountainsides, the birds and wild flowers all held my deepest attention. But, most of all, I fell hopelessly in love with the mountains, spending my summer vacations climbing the twisting mountain paths, armed only with my *clupaga*, and swimming in the cool mountain pools. My winter vacations I spent skiing down the snowy mountain slopes. Here, in this tiny mountain village, I spent some of the happiest days of my life.

# Chapter Two

## *Jesuits*

In Poland religion was of the highest importance, and to have a priest in the family was considered to be a great honour, particularly when the family was large, as ours was. I had six brothers and two sisters. During my final years at high school, my parents had been mapping out my adult life, unbeknownst to me. They had consulted the parish priest, who, considering my excellent school progress, concluded that I would be a good candidate for the priesthood. My parents had hinted at their ambitions for me over the years but my responses had been ambivalent. Failing to give a definite 'No' added fuel to the fire and roused their expectations.

During my last six months at high school, I arrived home one night to be greeted by my parents, the parish priest, and a physically large, devout-looking but rather forbidding man, who seemed to look down on me. He turned out to be the head of the Jesuit Seminary at Nowy Sacz.

My future was decided that evening during an informal discussion. I had a great thirst for knowledge and did not want to spend the rest of my life in Rudnik. Moreover, I was tempted by the promises of skiing in winter and tennis in summer, and living in the idyllic Nowy Sacz, on the banks of the river Dunajec. In addition, it was classed as a great honour to be accepted at the seminary even though my parents had to pay a considerable sum of money for the privilege. At that point I was too young to understand the personal sacrifice involved in becoming a priest or the implications of the Jesuit life. I had never thought of girls and the so-called facts of life had never been discussed at home.

At the seminary, discipline was much stricter than in the high school and the educational demands were greater than in an ordinary college. Studying and the reading of books selected and approved by the Jesuits took priority. Recreational activity such as chess, tennis and skiing was only permitted for two hours a day, usually during the early evening. I had no difficulty studying languages, Latin, Greek and German coming easily to me. In fact, while other students pored over their books, I became bored, having long since realised that I had a photographic memory and was able to absorb facts very easily. Boredom rekindled my urge to abscond. Often, instead of going to class, I would sneak off down to the river and spend the afternoon swimming in the cool waters of the Dunajec. On my return I would be called into the prefects' study and warned about my misdemeanours. These warnings having no effect, I was eventually deprived of my freedom. I was denied any leisure time and had to report to the study after every lesson for the rest of the school term.

I studied at the seminary for four years, returning to Rudnik only during the vacations. My brothers and sisters were making more demands on the family income and money was scarce. I found myself being pressurised to enter the monastery, even though I felt I had no vocation. The Jesuit fathers knew about my indecision and were very patient, hoping that a little pressure from my parents would persuade me to join them. Most students in the seminary took the vows as a matter of course. Although I had excelled at my studies, mainly to satisfy my parents' wishes, I was full of life and could see no reason why I should be forced into joining the monastery. However, the Jesuits knew how to handle hot-headed students and slowly but surely, with their powerful but gentle methods of persuasion, they began to turn my thoughts towards a life of serving God. They forced me to think about the work of God, and the honour bestowed on me and my family if I answered the call and gave myself up to the Lord. There would be

6

no worries about money, food, clothing and accommodation. Most important of all, I should be guaranteed Eternal Salvation.

These prospects began to look more attractive as time passed, especially for a young man who had not had any experience of the opposite sex. During the four-year period of study, the students went through a process of elimination and only the best were allowed to stay on and enter the Jesuit Order. At the start of my last term, my parents received a letter confirming that I had won my place.

I was at the crossroads of my life. My father sent me on holiday to Zakopane, high in the Tatra mountains, and there I debated the issue. To refuse the opportunity to serve God would be a grave disappointment to my parents who had worked hard to educate me and had set their hopes on having a priest in the family. Surely it was my duty to repay them. Although I knew I had no vocation, simple curiosity, a spirit of adventure and the thought of entering into the unknown all played their part in helping me to come to a decision. On my return from Zakopane, I travelled with my mother to Kalwaria, a shrine to the Holy Mary in the Benedictine monastery there and a place which thousands of pilgrims visited each year to pray for guidance. I knelt at the shrine, losing myself in prayer, my mind and body numb. It seemed that God wanted me to become a monk. He had led me to the shrine and had helped me to make my decision. I returned to my mother, kissed her hand and told her I had decided to enter the Jesuit monastery. We returned home to find that my father had already filled in the appropriate forms in anticipation of my answer. Two months passed before I received my acceptance.

In my new status as aspirant I would be on three months' probation, after which I could be accepted as a novice. Two more years of study would qualify me to take my perpetual vows. If I chose I could resign at that stage. However, once the vows were taken, I would have to live behind the monastery walls for the rest of my life. I read and re-read the letter but its true implications were lost on me, overridden by my sense of adventure and my impending journey into the unknown.

The next two weeks were hectic and emotional. My mother spent hours labelling all my belongings with my name and the number 22, which was my personal monastery number. As I said farewell to all my friends and relatives, they embraced me and spoke of the honour bestowed on our family by my acceptance into the Jesuit Order. With my belongings packed into two suitcases, my parents took me, in our cart, to the railway station. Here, on the platform, with tears streaming down my face, I kissed my mother and father goodbye and thanked them for all the sacrifices they had made for me.

I was soon on my way to Stara Wies in the south of Poland to start a new life, giving up my body and soul to the Jesuits, another inexperienced youth willing to become an obedient servant, ready to follow every instruction and resigned to living a life of chastity.

# Chapter Three

## *Life in the Monastery*

Life behind the monastery walls was nothing like I had anticipated. The first three months were spent under the careful eye of a specially appointed ascetic spiritual father. He assessed my character, giving me menial tasks to perform, like cleaning toilets and washing and polishing floors. Sometimes, after a full morning's work, I would return from lunch to find water emptied all over my polished floor. I was expected to dry and polish the floor again without a word. I gritted my teeth and pretended that nothing could break my patience and obedience. I convinced them. Three months to the day after my arrival, I received my Jesuit tunic and was accepted into the noviciate.

The life of the novice was one of unvarying routine. At five o'clock in the morning, to the sound of the monastery bell, I got up and went to the assembly rooms for one hour's meditation, the points of the meditation having been provided by the spiritual father the previous evening. Mass and Holy Communion followed. After this we were allowed to eat. Four hours' solid study came next, and then lunch. We were then allowed one hour's recreation, which we usually spent playing chess or table tennis. Somewhat refreshed, we then attended to the general duties or chores that had been assigned to us. Our academic day ended with two hours of reading, bible studies, Latin and ascetic books. During the evening the Master of Novices would issue his instructions for the following morning's meditation. We ended the day with long religious debates which lasted until the sound of the monastery bell summoned us to our beds.

The Novice Master was my spiritual and moral adviser. It was my responsibility to open my heart to him, to discuss my problems and temptations and to ask his advice on anything that was worrying me. I found I could not be sincere with him, especially when he suggested different bodily punishments for my temptations. Sexual temptations were dealt with by flagellation. The flagella, or whip, made of five leather thongs fastened together and knotted at the end, was drawn across your back while you recited the psalm *De profundis clamavi*. Sometimes, during the recreation periods, the Novice Master would enter the room unexpectedly, calling all the students present to a debate. One poor fellow would be singled out as needing spiritual help. He would kneel before the Master, kiss the floor and recite *Carissimi Patres et Fratres Peto Eleumusinam Spiritualem*, meaning 'Dearest fathers and brothers, give me spiritual help'. The student, still kneeling, would be interrogated about his sins as if in a court of law. Admitted misdemeanours would receive a penalty. Light punishment meant cleaning out the toilets and kitchen during the recreation period. Heavy punishment involved lying prostrate on the hard floor, legs together and arms outstretched for one hour. Any movement at all would mean that the prostration would have to resume the following day, and every day until the whole hour had been spent totally immobile.

It was a strict, hard life. Students were bullied and punished for trivial offences and many left the monastery before their noviciate was completed and they had to take the perpetual vows of obedience, chastity and poverty. I was stubborn and not the type to give in to harassment. I had a strong will which seemed to grow stronger with the treatment I received.

As the date of my perpetual vows drew near, my mind was once more in a turmoil. During the probationary period we were constantly reminded about God's severity, and how sinning against God would mean eternal banishment. This rigorous doctrine was never tempered by mention of the love and mercy of the Almighty. We, the chosen few, would attain eternal salvation only if we believed in God's severity and became totally submissive to His will. Passing through the gates of heaven was like getting through the eye of the proverbial needle. It was naturally with some trepidation that I finally agreed to take my vows.

Yet, having done so, I found myself in a whole new world with much more freedom. I was sent, with a handful of other students who had survived the noviciate, to the Jesuit Scholasticat on the River Pina in eastern Poland. This was the first time I had been outside the walls for two years. There was an immediate improvement: the atmosphere was more relaxed, the educational standards improved, leisure time became more abundant. The past two years had been thoroughly depressing and I looked forward to life in the Scholasticat with great anticipation. Unfortunately for me, there were temptations on every side.

For example, sailing was permitted on the stretch of the Pina near the monastery walls. Beautiful girls swam in the cool waters and sunbathed on the river bank. Older, more mature students acted as our guardians, teaching us to 'observe the modesty of our eyes'. But though I tried to avert my eyes, curiosity prevailed and for the first time in my life I felt the stirring of desire awaken in my body. Needless to say I was still a virgin and my sex education had been nil. I had never thought about the opposite sex, being too absorbed in my education and spiritual welfare. My life in the monastery had indoctrinated me into fighting all temptations. But now doubts started to assail me. Had God created me to be a kind of mechanical robot, devoid of all sexual feelings? Though I had taken my vows, my body had not changed and I was still the same person beneath my monk's habit. For the first time I began to question the vow of chastity.

My constant thoughts on this subject caused my studies to suffer and progress came to a halt. My nights were spent dreaming about the beautiful girls on the banks of the Pina. No longer naive about sexual matters, I transported myself into their bedrooms and invariably woke the following mornings having had a 'wet dream'. This was classed as a heavy sin which I had to confess before taking Holy Communion each morning. This, my one and only sin, was confessed most mornings on a regular basis. Normal confessions are private and confidential but in a monastery this convention is not observed.

Eventually I was summoned to the office for an interview with my Spiritual Father who degraded me, called me unclean and unholy and accused me of being worse than an animal and unfit to wear the monk's robe. I was ordered to kneel before the cross for twelve hours and to pray to God to purify my thoughts. This had the opposite effect to the one intended, adding fuel to the fire. My thoughts began, almost inexorably, to turn away from the Church.

Over the next few months I worked out what I thought was a logical philosophy. Surely, according to religion, God created me in His own image, designing my body for a purpose. Not to use my body for that purpose was contrary to nature and automatically against the will of the Creator. I was surrounded by people who claimed to love God but at the same time rejected the most essential element of His creation, without which the human race could not continue to exist. I felt that the rule of celibacy was created by a generation of monks who wished to keep an upper hand over their subordinates. I was aware that other Christian churches did not maintain the rule of celibacy, allowing their members to use their bodies in the way that God intended. In my studies of the scriptures I tried, unsuccessfully, to find passages supporting the Jesuits' interpretation of their doctrine.

Having arranged an interview with my superiors, I put forward my views. Unfortunately my logical philosophy clashed with the teachings of the Church. It was, I was told, a grave sin to even think about the opposite sex and to engage in any sexual activity meant condemnation by the Creator to eternal torment. I was advised to think again, whilst being assured that many students went through a period of 'unrest'. I was reminded of my vows and of my promise to sacrifice my normal life for God. These words stayed with me through my entire life. More than anything in the world I wanted to be relieved of my vows and to resume a normal life. A kind of claustrophobia took possession of me. I felt like a trapped animal. The only answer, said my superiors, was prayer. On the contrary, I came to the conclusion that God could not be wrong. Since I had followed his scriptures, I was not wrong either.

It was at this time that I started to look for a substitute. I began to feel desire when I was with one of my fellow students. He was angelic, rather womanly in his mannerisms. I would watch him undress by the river, following him with my eyes as he swam in the cool waters. Sometimes I would touch him accidently as we both swam. For a time I was happy in my fantasy. I did not reveal my feelings for fear of being rebuffed. If he had responded to my loving gazes my life would have been totally changed and I would have become a homosexual.

Eventually my misery became so acute that I thought of throwing myself from the bell tower. But the thought of punishment, if I lived, deterred me. I knew that if I died I would be damned to eternal hell for taking my own life. I abandoned the idea. In desperation one afternoon, I went to see the Magister of Biology, a kindly man of around seventy. I needed someone to give me spiritual stability. I sat with him in his study for two hours pouring out my heart to him while he listened in silence. Eventually he responded.

'You have a vivid imagination, my son, but you are not alone. Most of us have had difficulties like yours at some time in our lives. God knows about your suffering here on the earth and He will reward you with eternal freedom and peace after your death. Be patient, since these feelings will soon pass. I was well into my third decade before I found peace of mind, but it will come for you as it did for me. Gain your strength in prayer and direct your desires into your studies. I will pray for your guidance.'

I kissed his hands, and looked into the eyes of this sad, seventy-year-old man. I saw myself in the years to come. Did I really want to stay in the monastery for the rest of my life like this man or did I want to break with the Jesuits and start a new life whilst I was still young and strong? I took my decision and sleep came easily that night.

# Chapter Four

## *The Escape*

It was a fine spring day the day I decided to leave the monastery. I had weighed up the consequences. Breaking my perpetual vows would mean my excommunication from the Church. My parents, whom I had not seen since that day, now long ago, when they had taken me to the railway station, would be unbearably disappointed. Yet I refused to weaken. I went to the monastery chapel for the last time, and knelt in front of the statue of the Holy Mary to beg her forgiveness. For three solid hours I prayed, my tears flowing freely. My face became puffed and red.

As dawn began to break, I left the chapel and walked along the corridor to my room. The bell had sounded and the dormitories were alive with noise. My seventy-year-old magister was walking towards me. He touched my arm, looked into my eyes, saw my red puffed-up face and in those brief seconds I knew he could read my mind.

'May God be with you, my son, whatever you may have decided to do. I will pray for you.'

He released my arm and I was alone, on what would be my last day in the monastery. I dressed at 3 o'clock the next morning, having sat up half the night planning my escape. I thought two hours would give plenty of time to be far away from the monastery gates. The walls were two metres high, with sharp pieces of broken glass cemented into the top. This was not so much to keep the monks in as to keep trespassers from stealing the fruit and vegetables from the monastery gardens. Wearing my monk's clothing (my civilian clothing had long since gone), I donned my long heavy coat and crept out of the dormitory. In the garden behind the greenhouses the monks stored the ladders which were used during the late summer to collect the fruit from the trees. I used one of these to scale the wall.

Being unfamiliar with the surrounding countryside, I decided that the best plan would be to stick to the railway, which ran from Lwów in the south through Pinsk to Wilno in the north. The cattle trucks were standing in the sidings waiting to be picked up by the goods train that morning. Taking off my monastery gown, my white stiff collar and my broad belt, I hid them underneath the hay in one of the wagons facing south. Putting on my long heavy coat once more, I picked my way across the railway lines to the wagons waiting to go north. Now the deed was done, I panicked. Would my clothes be discovered before the train started its journey? Would they see through my false trail? Had my disappearance been discovered? Were they already searching for me?

I squeezed myself between the bales of hay. It was dawn; soon the engine would arrive, couple up and take me to Wilno to a new life. I now had time to think about my situation. Though every station was a station further away from the Jesuits, I had no clear idea of my destination. I could not go home since the monks would get in touch with my parents as soon as I was reported missing. I had no clothes, no money, no food. Perhaps anyone else in this situation would have given in, and returned with their tail between their legs, asking for forgiveness. But I was determined not to go back. I had made the break. The life of a nomad was more desirable than the life of a monk.

I remembered that I had an uncle in Stolpce, a town on the Polish–Russian border on the River Nemen. He was a sergeant in the army and had strongly objected to my joining the Jesuits, asking my father to consider sending me into the army instead. The train was heading roughly in the right direction. Now, with added enthusiasm, I ventured out of my hiding place each time the train slowed down, hoping to catch a glimpse of the approaching station so as to work out my position. But the darkness and the gentle rocking of the wagon made me lose all sense of direction and time. Eventually the train pulled into Baronovichi. I knew that Stolpce was about 40 miles to the east and this was the best place to leave the train. I waited until it began to pick up speed after leaving the station, and then jumped. My usually springy legs gave way on impact and I rolled over and over down the embankment. For what seemed like hours I lay still, gasping for breath.

The air smelt of pine forests. I stood up to absorb the panoramic view spread out before me. The land was covered with forest as far as the eye could see. The sun was now high in the sky and I was free. This was my true way of life. Nature had called me back to her bosom. I began my journey in an easterly direction along a rutted and stony forest track. Since I had only possessed open-toed sandals in the monastery, my feet were not shod for walking any distance. Soon I was glad to see a peasant cart coming towards me bringing a family returning to Baronovichi from some local market place. This reminded me of happy childhood days and tears welled in my eyes. I beckoned to the family and asked if I was on the right track for Stolpce but they swore at me, made the sign of the cross and hurried away, Looking down at myself, I understood why they had been afraid. My long coat covered in straw (it was May and the temperature was high), the cuts on my feet, and my unkempt hair must have conveyed an impression of wildness and vagrancy.

By early evening I began to feel despondent. I was tired, hungry (I had not eaten for 24 hours) and my encounter with the family of peasants had deterred me from calling at the small farms nestling on the edge of the forest. My coat was heavy but much more respectable than the underpants and vest I wore underneath. Suddenly I heard the sound of flowing water, music to my ears. In front of me was a rickety wooden bridge over a stream of crystal-clear water. Like a man possessed I flung myself into the coolness, dousing my hair and face, soaking my blistered feet and quenching my thirst. Sourbelly grew on the banks of the stream and I ate lustily, remembering the days I had run home complaining of stomach ache after eating too much of it. My hunger disappeared and I began to relax. Before fatigue overcame me I tried to pray. I promised to atone for my sins if only I was allowed to survive this ordeal. Before I fell asleep a desperate feeling of loneliness flowed over me. What could I say to my uncle, assuming he still lived in Stolpce? How could I face my mother and father? Could I approach the Jesuits to beg their forgiveness and seek official release from my vows? If they refused I would suffer excommunication and become an outcast. I would have no right to work, no right to marry and above all no right to be buried in consecrated ground.

When dawn came I drank more of the cool water and continued on my way. I walked for miles, knowing that if I stopped I would collapse at the side of the road. Eventually another cart came into view, this time approaching me from the rear. Stepping into the ditch to let it pass, I was surprised to see two soldiers. They reined the horses to a halt and looked me up and down in distaste. Thinking I was a beggar, they jumped off the cart and began to ridicule me. In desperation I mentioned my Uncle Ludwik, asking how many more miles to Stolpce. The baiting stopped. They were unsure of themselves, not knowing what to make of me. They began to ask questions – where had I come from, where was my uncle stationed, why was I dressed like a vagrant? I answered them honestly. They looked at one another. They were heading for Stolpce which was about 10 kilometres away and, if I was who I said I was, they would take me to my uncle.

Conversation was non-stop. The soldiers were curious about the Jesuits and my bid for freedom. Questions came thick and fast. Time passed quickly and soon the forests gave way to fields and farms and I could see houses and a church in the distance. I had arrived in Stolpce. I recognised my uncle's house as I drew up in the narrow street. My companions were still unsure of me; after all, if I was a vagrant and not the person I claimed to be, they would get into serious trouble for picking up a stranger in the forest. I suggested that I stay in the cart until my uncle was found.

It was with bated breath that I waited for him to appear. I was unsure of his reaction to seeing his nephew looking like a pauper. My fears were groundless. Rushing towards me, he hugged me to his chest, and quickly made preparations for me to wash, to receive some proper clothes and to be given a good meal in his house. In the evening I told my uncle and aunt the whole story. He was amazed at my adventures but he agreed with my reasons for leaving the monastery, reminding me that he had opposed my father's decision to persuade me to become a Jesuit. Despite my anxiety, he postponed all decisions until the morning. Before going to bed I hugged him and thanked him for taking me into his house and caring for me.

It was mid-morning before I woke. My uncle had not gone to his duties and was waiting for me when I finally rose. We discussed my problem for over an hour, trying to work out the best solution. Finally he suggested that I write to the Jesuits explaining my reasons for absconding, humbling myself and begging their forgiveness. I should request them to rescind my perpetual vows and plead with them not to have me excommunicated. I should explain that I had not been mature enough to take my vows when I did and I had only done so because I had no wish to embarrass my parents by changing my mind at the last minute, after they had put so much effort and time into sending me to the monastery.

His second suggestion was that I write a long letter to my parents informing them that I was safe and begging their forgiveness. I should acknowledge that I had let them down and that I was ashamed, but nothing on earth would persuade me to return to the monastery life.

The letter I received from my parents filled me with elation. They were relieved that I was safe. They expressed no anger and urged me to return to Rudnik. However, I decided to stay with my uncle until the reply from the monastery arrived, which took well over a month.

The reason for the delay was that the General of the Jesuits,

Father Ledochowski, resided in Rome and had to be informed by letter of my behaviour. A council was held and my problems were discussed. They offered to absolve me from my perpetual vows and to take away the threat of excommunication. But first I had to present myself before a panel of Elders who would see me in neighbouring Grodno. This suited me since I felt it would be safer than going back to the monastery.

My legs were trembling as I entered the building owned by the monks, which closely resembled the monastery on the River Pina. The delegation from the Scholasticat had been held up en route and eventually arrived weary from their long journey. They were not amused. Why had I absconded? Was it not obvious that my unreasonable behaviour would cause a scandal? Why had I not approached someone to discuss my problems? The grilling continued for a long time. I was told there were precedents for monks to be released from their vows, but I would have to confess before the ceremony of absolution could be performed. To this I readily agreed and was taken to a small chapel in the grounds where I confessed. My soul purified, I was taken back to the delegation whereupon the absolution was performed. A weight fell from my heart. At last I was free!

I now found it very difficult to look at a member of the opposite sex without exploding with sexual desire, so, for many months, I continued to observe the 'modesty of my eyes'. My parents were anxious for me to return home and so it was with mixed feelings that I packed my few belongings (almost all gifts of my aunt and uncle) and embarked on my long journey home. But going back in time is never a good idea and after the initial happiness of actually seeing me safe and well, my parents returned to their daily tasks as if nothing had happened. However, I felt uncomfortable. People gave me furtive glances as they passed me in the street and our parish priest was very cool, not looking me in the eye when we happened to meet. Most of my old friends were respectably married with families of their own. I began to feel like a social outcast. I was reluctant to become totally dependent on my father, so I decided to find work in Kraków until I was called up for compulsory army service. I found a job as a gardener and then as a waiter in a large restaurant. I gradually responded to normal life. Suddenly I realised that the 'modesty of my eyes' was becoming a thing of the past.

# Chapter Five

## *The Army*

I was overjoyed to receive my orders to report for my army medical examination. This was what I had been waiting for. I was passed physically fit and ordered to report for duty with the 13th Regiment of Cavalry in Nowa Vilejka in the north of Poland. However, I found the early part of my army career rather a trial. Though I was used to strictness and had no problem with education, I found it very hard to mix with the ordinary peasant soldiers. Their behaviour and sometimes obscene and vulgar language was uncongenial and I never really adapted myself to their ways.

During my monastery life, I had perfected my game of chess and was constantly on the lookout for new opponents. Since these were few and far between among the peasant soldiers, I was delighted to be invited to play against the Captain, who was reputed to be extremely good. He was good but I managed to beat him and he became my regular opponent. After our games he would offer me a glass of vodka and the conversation would get around to my career. We discussed at some length my escape from the Jesuits. The Captain thought that the fearlessness I had shown was one of the important qualities of a good commanding officer. I was also well-educated. Why not apply for the signals course at Grodno when my two years' compulsory service ended? I could see no objection. Army life was quite palatable and my uncle seemed to enjoy it. So, six weeks later I was on my way to Grodno where I took several signals courses, passing each one with flying colours. Returning to my unit, I was immediately promoted to corporal.

This restored my family's faith in me and they were full of admiration for my two stripes. At the end of a short visit home, I applied to serve for five years in the Air Force Meteorological Service. At the beginning of 1939 I was accepted, but international events pushed me in a very different direction.

It was becoming increasingly obvious to many of us that, after the events in Czechoslovakia in 1938 and 1939, Poland would be the next of Hitler's victims. I remember the enormous enthusiasm of my fellow soldiers on hearing the news that Hitler might be planning an onslaught on Poland. What folly! We were still recovering from the previous war, trying to rebuild our economy. Germany's armoured strength and the number of her fighting planes far exceeded ours. When the day of mobilisation arrived we had to give up our sabres for sharpening; were these the weapons we were to use to attack German tanks? Again, after we had cleaned our rifles for inspection, we were each given our ration of twenty bullets; that was all. We were ordered to shoot to kill and if in any doubt about hitting the target, to hold our fire, since bullets were precious. How could we be a match for German automatic weapons armed with abundant ammunition? However, we sang patriotic songs of the Polish army to keep our spirit up and we showed no fear as we loaded our horses onto the trains making for the Polish–German border.

Our cavalry regiment, accompanied by anti-tank guns, was sent to the front line, where we managed to destroy eight German tanks before our ammunition ran out. The German Panzers then pushed us back towards the Vistula and we were subjected to constant artillery fire. Though we fought like lions, there was no escape and we had no alternative but to swim the river with our horses, all the bridges having been destroyed by Polish sappers. Many of our soldiers could not swim. As they fought to stay above the water, they were dispatched at will by the Luftwaffe. The Vistula was full of the bloodied bodies of men and horses.

My friend Janek and I were more fortunate, reaching the opposite bank complete with our rifles, sabres and horses. We fled to the forest for shelter, where we attempted to regroup with other survivors. We discovered that at least half of our regiment had been wiped out and most of our remaining ammunition was lost in the river. Though our spirits were still quite high, we hoped above all for a period of rest before the German tanks crossed the river and once again began their onslaught. Unfortunately they were on us again before we could organise a substantial and coordinated defence. So we took to guerrilla warfare, lying low during the daytime and attacking the German forces after dark. We used to split up into small groups, gaining an element of surprise in our attacks. These tactics became the model for the subsequent Polish Underground Army, which remained an effective force throughout the war. About this time, differences of opinion began to surface in the regiment, some wanting to surrender and take the consequences but the majority wishing to continue the fight, even though we knew it was useless. We then learned that we were almost entirely surrounded and that the Soviet army had advanced into the eastern provinces of our country, cutting off our retreat in that direction. Some Polish regiments had successfully crossed the Hungarian frontier, or so rumour had it. It quickly became every man for himself in this game of survival. Our regiment ceased to exist.

Janek and I decided to make for home together since he lived only some thirty miles from Rudnik, my own village. Since we were out of food, we used to collect turnips and potatoes from the fields at dusk, eating them raw. Our only possessions were the clothes we stood up in, our rifles, a handful of bullets and our horses. During the day, we took refuge in the forest, venturing out only when we knew it was safe. Most of the farms en route had been abandoned, their owners in such haste to escape the German advance that they left behind their animals and most of their belongings. During the nights most of these farms were taken over by German soldiers for accommodation, so it was unwise to approach them.

At last we came upon a farm where the farmer and his wife were openly tending their hens and geese. There was no sign of German occupation. When night fell we ventured down to the farmhouse. I tapped quickly on the door while Janek scoured the darkness for any movement. We heard footsteps inside and the sound of bolts being drawn back. When the farmer saw two soldiers on his doorstep a look of sheer terror crossed his face. I whispered to him in Polish that we were not Germans and tried to show him our uniforms in the shaft of light given by the lath of spruce burning beneath the chimney.

'I can't let you stay here,' he whispered. 'They have taken my cows and pigs and my horses. My wife is not well and she can't walk far. In return for provisions the Germans are letting us stay but they visit us regularly. There is a German base two kilometres down the road. They're biding their time waiting for their orders to come through.'

It was obvious that our arrival had placed them in danger. The old man was shaking as he spoke and I noticed his wife trying to hide in the corner of the room behind a sheaf of straw. I explained that all we wanted was civilian clothing and some food in exchange for our horses and equipment. He was too frightened to agree but eventually his wife, after conferring with him quietly, came to our aid.

'We will help you. It's a sad day when we cannot help two of our countrymen.'

The farmer, still muttering under his breath, found us two pairs of trousers, a long coat, a jacket, and two worn shirts. We immediately dug a large hole in his garden and buried our uniforms and equipment in a large box. There was a haystack in the field nearest the forest which the Germans had checked out several days before. The farmer thought we would be relatively safe during the day hiding in the stack; if we were caught he would deny all knowledge of us. For a week we rested in the haystack and under cover of darkness he would bring us boiled potatoes and eggs. We felt like beggars.

Finally news came that the Germans were on the move. We hid

in the stack for two more days, not daring to venture out until we were sure that every tank had passed through. After that we were quickly on our way, mingling on the road with peasants heading home to their farms and villages. They took us for one of themselves. We picked up information that many young people had been captured and sent to Germany to work in the coal and steel industries. Jews had been rounded up and sent to concentration camps. These stories made our blood run cold but gave us an incentive to get back to our respective villages and be reunited with our families. However, we decided that in the circumstances it would be safer to travel only at night.

The journey from Opol to Tarnow and Bochnia took five days. Nothing untoward happened to us and we found travelling during the night quite easy. After two more days we reached Myslenice, the nearest town to Rudnik, where we parted company. We hugged each other sadly, not knowing what fate had in store for us. I watched the lonely figure of Janek disappear from view before turning to follow my own road to Rudnik.

# Chapter Six

## *The Search*

Rudnik was like a ghost town, the usually busy streets deserted and the houses locked and boarded. I knew deep down inside that my parents' house would be empty too, and so it proved. A large padlock secured the door. When a villager approached, I asked him what had happened, why it was so quiet and if he knew where my family had gone. He shrugged his shoulders. Apparently a German officer had been shot close to the church. Immediately the Gestapo had rounded up what remained of the menfolk and herded them into the village square. Having manhandled them, pushing and shoving them into line, the soldiers then chose fifteen for public execution. This was my first experience of what the Germans called 'pacification'.

As for my family, they had travelled east to stay with relatives. He suggested that I go to Sulkowice where some of my relatives had remained. I remembered hearing on my last leave that my Uncle Ludwik and Aunt Olenka had moved to Sulkowice from Stolpce. There, in the village of his birth, they had built themselves a pleasant house where they hoped to retire. It was on this door that I eventually knocked. My aunt was overjoyed to see me safe and well. But my uncle was away at the war, as were most of the menfolk in my family. She begged me to stay. Since my journey had been long and fraught, I decided to remain at least for the night. But I was no nearer to being reunited with my immediate family and I had an uneasy feeling that something was wrong.

When I had rested and eaten and changed into some decent

clothes my aunt found for me, I had to decide what to do. My aunt pleaded with me to stay since my mother and father would almost certainly arrive there shortly. Moreover, I could speak German, which would be of great use to the villagers who needed a translator and a leader to help them through their difficulties. Though tempted by my aunt's appeal, my thoughts were continually with my parents. My mother, being of Austrian origin, could speak German and should have been safe under German rule, but I still had a nagging feeling that something was wrong. I knew I had to find them if only for my own peace of mind.

I found out from the villagers that the Germans' main headquarters were in Kraków. Here you could apply in person for a *Bescheinigung Karte*, a document given to Poles who could speak German and were in a position to assist the Germans in running the country. Possession of this pass permitted the holder to move freely in German-occupied Poland. Against my aunt's wishes I travelled to Kraków the following day.

The thought of entering German headquarters terrified me. I knew I was taking a great risk. However, cultivating my best German accent, I asked to see the *Oberst* who, to my surprise, agreed to interview me. Sitting in his office I felt extremely vulnerable knowing that he could have me arrested or even shot without further question. Trying to keep my German accent perfect, I outlined why I wanted an identity card and of course conveyed the information that my mother was Austrian, born in the South Tyrol and that her maiden name was Schweiz. In short I needed a card to travel east to find my parents and bring them back to Rudnik.

He stared at me, fingers clasped together, hands resting on his chin.

'I sympathise. I'm of Austrian origin myself. I'm sure your parents are safe but I understand your concern. Actually there's no reason why I should give you an ID. If I were you I wouldn't risk leaving your village. But don't let it be said that we are unsympathetic. Your German's excellent and it could be put to good use since we're in need of interpreters. But, if you wish to find your family, I'll arrange for you to have a pass.'

He stood up. I thought my legs would collapse as I rose to my feet. We shook hands.

'Bring your mother to see me if you return home to Rudnik with her. A little light conversation with a person from my homeland would raise my spirits.'

As I turned to leave, he pressed something into my hand, saying it was a little something to help me on my journey. It was not until I had my identity card safely in my pocket that I opened my hand and found, crumpled up in my palm, fifty German marks.

Jubilantly I returned to Sulkowice. Back at my aunt's house I was so excited about my pass that I picked up my aunt and danced her around the room. Now I could move without fear. That evening I planned my journey to Przemysl, a town on the demarcation line between the German and Soviet-occupied areas of Poland, through which ran the river San. The town was split down the middle, with German soldiers on the west bank and Soviet troops on the east. Despite these unusual circumstances, life seemed to be going on as usual. But for me the centre of attention was the bridge which connected the two banks of the river. If I were to enter the Soviet-occupied area this seemed to be my only route.

A huge market was in progress on the west bank. I watched the bridge and the market for two hours but didn't see one person cross the bridge or venture up to the four soldiers on guard outside the makeshift sentry boxes on the access path. Tanks lurked in the background, not quite out of sight, their guns pointing east. Perhaps it was easy to cross the bridge after all. Since I had the correct documents and could speak perfect German, I decided to try.

As I approached one of the soldiers, his three companions raised their guns in readiness. My pass was inspected and everything seemed to be in order.

'What is your business on the east side?'

I told him briefly why I wished to cross over. Though he sympathised, his answer was a definite no.

'It's for your own good. The Russians won't let you pass since your papers mean nothing to them. Siberia next stop!'

I did not like to be beaten but it was obvious that these soldiers were not prepared to let me pass and I would be pushing my luck to press them further. I decided to stay in Przemysl for a few days to get to know a few of the locals and to find out how the Polish Jews were managing to get out of the area to escape Hitler and the German atrocities we had heard about.

I sat in the café every day, but the only conversations were about the feeding of cattle and pigs, how much wheat could be bought and the price of fresh fruit and vegetables. I was certainly becoming an agricultural expert but was sadly short of information about how to cross the bridge. Eventually I took to wandering round the market making furtive enquiries but this tactic was not successful either until the fourth day. Then the penny dropped with one of the market traders. Get in touch with the 'beggar' was the gist of his advice; for a small consideration, this 'beggar' could probably put me in touch with someone who could help. With that the trader moved off, not wanting to arouse the suspicion of the German soldiers.

I wandered round the market looking for the beggar. It was late afternoon before I saw him sitting near the pig pens, a large sack over his shoulder, a cracked mug in his hand, reaching out as people passed and asking them to spare a little money. In fact I had seen him many times before, begging food and drink from the market traders. It was difficult to believe that this was the man who could help me. I soon put him to the test. Putting one Polish zloty in his mug, I remained standing near him. Noticing I had not moved, he eventually asked if there was something he could do for me. Quickly I told him my story.

He smiled, still not looking directly at me. He then explained in a very cultured Polish accent that he was an agent for the Jews and that there was an organised 'pass point' at one of the small villages close to the river between Przemysl and Jaroslaw. A villager with a boat would take people over for $25. The price was high but the risk was considerable. Anyway, the Jews had the money and were willing to pay a high price for freedom. He fell silent and I knew it would take another zloty to get him to reveal the name of the village and the name of my contact. That was a minor problem compared with raising $25, which was an impossible sum for me. Even the money I had started out with was disappearing fast. Nevertheless I decided to find the crossing point.

I had to make the journey in darkness since the road was much too dangerous. German motorcycles patrolled at irregular intervals. Keeping close to the river bank offered a solution but brought with it additional hazards since the terrain was mainly swampland. The best course, I decided, was to follow a line of willow trees which, though slightly inland, followed the natural course of the river and promised to be firmer under foot. In this way, travelling in the dark and stopping for food in the tiny villages during the day, I reached the vicinity of the crossing in two days. Searching the area, I quite unexpectedly came upon a boat, half hidden and a short distance from the river.

My first instinct was to steal the boat and row hell for leather for the opposite bank. But since it was broad daylight I would be a sitting target for German or Soviet patrols. With plenty of time on my hands, I wandered into the local village to wait for darkness. I decided I would return to the crossing point at dusk, hide in the undergrowth until there were signs of movement and then, when the escapees were ready to board, dash out and demand free passage across the river. Since I had no spare money, this was the only way I could think of to get across.

I waited three long nights before my vigil paid off. I heard the rustle of leaves and the noise of something heavy being dragged down the embankment. I moved to within hearing distance of the figures huddled in conversation. It was a cloudy night, with no moon. This was my chance. I sprang from my hiding place, confronted the boatman and ordered him to take me across the river. Ranting and raving about my family, I acted like a man possessed. But my insistence, though stunning the group into silence, had little more effect. The boat was already overcrowded; all the people had paid their money; I could be no exception. I panicked.

'You will all suffer if I cannot go with you.'

Saying which, I started to run frenziedly towards the main road. The Jews, fearful that German patrols would hear the commotion, chased after me and brought me to the ground. After berating me for my stupidity in putting so many lives at risk, they offered to pay my passage in the hope that I would stop acting like an enemy. Now thoroughly contrite I apologised, explaining that my behaviour had been brought on by panic, fatigue and the suspense of waiting for so long. After a few discreet words the boatman agreed, against his better judgement, to allow me on board.

The darkness was ominous, the journey endless even though the river was only thirty metres wide, and the boat extremely cramped with ten passengers in a space designed for six. I tried to work out a cover story for the Soviet guards in case I was stopped. I decided to say that I was seeking Soviet protection after escaping from the brutality of the German occupation and that I hoped to be reunited with my family, who had already escaped to Soviet territory. I could not tell whether this approach would be successful.

# Chapter Seven

## *Encounter with the Soviet Authorities*

Understandably, the boatman was extremely nervous. He had made regular ferry journeys with Jews since the start of the German occupation and had made a good deal of money. The risk was normally high but tonight's commotion had increased it and all he wanted to do was to land his passengers as quickly as possible and set off home. Eight Jews, a paltry assortment of belongings and I were deposited hastily on the eastern bank.

I decided to help the man who had paid my fare to reach the road. In the pitch darkness it was difficult to avoid the marshes and river bogs. The undergrowth was dense and the only path leading away from the river was very overgrown. In our eagerness to find the road, we never thought about the noise, the snapping of twigs and the rustling of leaves and branches echoing in the night stillness.

At last we emerged onto the road from the shelter of the trees only to freeze in our tracks. Confronting us were seven soldiers, their hats decorated with the hammer and sickle. Still, we quickly recovered ourselves, expecting that they would protect us when they heard why we'd escaped. But they gave us no time to explain. To our immense surprise they seized us, held their bayonets against our throats, forced us into pairs and gave the order '*Poganiaj!*', which meant 'March!'. We 'marched' the three kilometres to the nearest village where the Soviets had taken over the large hall as their headquarters. The night was cold and wet and the dampness seeped through our clothing, but there was no warmth waiting for us in the village hall.

Ushered into an empty room, our baggage thrown in a heap, we were ordered to sit on the bare floor, our legs apart and our hands touching the floor between our knees. Two Soviet guards remained in the room whilst the remainder of the patrol returned to their post by the river, no doubt congratulating themselves on a good night's work. The two older Jews, aware of their dangerous position, hunched their shoulders and muttered prayers under their breath. The younger ones, overcome by fatigue after their long journey, fought to keep their eyes open. If they did drop off, they were rudely kicked awake by a Russian boot.

I remained alert trying to assess my position, hoping that in the morning I could speak to someone in authority. Having studied Russian in the monastery, I could understand and speak the language fluently, a fact which the soldiers were still unaware of. Permitted to smoke whilst guarding us, the pungent smell of their tobacco permeated the air. Laughing at our misery and discomfort, they punctuated their conversation with obscenities and crude jokes. One of them began making suggestions about the two women in our party, describing in detail what he would do to them if he thought he could get away with it.

Unable to move I began to get stomach cramps. Then my insides knotted and I began to vomit. This was highly entertaining to the soldiers who mocked me by copying my squatting position and going through the motions of being sick. Quickly tiring of this mimicry, they soon returned to their tobacco and their unpleasant jokes. I now realised, too late, that I could expect no mercy from the Russians. Crossing the river had been a dreadful mistake.

As dawn broke the older Jews became restless. Once again they resorted to bribery, having seen it work before. But their offers to the guards of gold watches and money this time fell on deaf ears.

'You have nothing, nothing of any value to us, not even your clothing belongs to you, you filthy capitalists. You will be set free, not in Poland but in the Siberian forests beyond the Urals', was the gist of the guards' reply.

Morning brought the arrival of the colonel. The guards stubbed out their cigarettes and smartened their uniforms, standing to attention when the door opened. Silhouetted in the doorway stood a man of about six feet, dressed in an immaculate uniform and wearing row after row of medals and stars on his chest. On each wrist he wore an expensive wristwatch. Behind him stood two other men, both members of the NKVD, the secret police of the USSR during the war. The three men stepped into the room. The NKVD men were dressed in bluish-grey uniforms, guns tucked into their belts, blue caps on their heads. They too, I was surprised to see, wore a wristwatch on each wrist; one of them was even wearing a compass. We were ordered to stand to attention. Having sat in the same position for at least ten hours, we found it extremely difficult to stand up and could only remain upright with the help of our guards. No conversation took place. The colonel stared at each of us, then turned and left the room as quickly as he had entered it. The soldiers, talking among themselves, mentioned the words, 'interrogation centre'. I presumed we would soon be sent for.

Eventually each person was ordered into the interrogation room separately, taking their belongings with them. Having been interrogated they had their possessions confiscated and became prisoners. They were all charged with trespassing over the temporary Russian border, having been arrested by the patrol during the hours of curfew. This was sufficient evidence under Soviet law to send them to labour camps for a minimum of ten years.

I was left until last. In the interrogation room three men were seated behind a long table and I was propelled in their direction by the bayonet of one of the guards. I remember to this day the colonel's first question.

'*Diengi?*\* On the table please.'

In my best Russian accent, I replied that I had no money. He was rather taken aback by my mastery of his language but even more surprised that I had no money. Holding out his hand, he

\* Money

asked for my identification papers. I stalled for time, hoping to hold on to my German ID for as long as possible. I explained why I had crossed the border. This was provocation: I was reminded that I had not 'crossed' the border but 'violated' it. I tried to continue the story but suddenly the colonel was on his feet, thumping the table with his fist.

'Enough! I am asking the questions, you capitalist swine. I have absolutely no interest in your tale of woe. Papers, now!'

The soldiers moved as if to search me. I had no option. I took the ID from my pocket and handed it to the colonel.

The impact of my German documents on the three men was unbelievable. They passed the papers from one to the other. The colonel first turned deathly pale, then glowed crimson red. They all three jabbered and laughed hysterically, acting like idiots. The colonel, finally, held up his hand for silence. With a look of triumph in his eyes, he turned to his companions.

'What we have here, gentlemen, is none other than a bastard German spy. Search him. Search the bastard.'

The soldiers, at last given the chance to behave like animals, tore off my clothing until I was standing naked in front of them. Apart from a few Polish zlotys and two German marks, they found nothing. Not satisfied, they tore the lining out of my jacket and, when they still could find nothing, threw my tattered clothing in a heap at my feet, telling me to cover my filthy German body.

Shivering, for the room was still extremely cold, I dressed myself, still pleading my innocence. For a moment I thought they were actually listening to me as I explained that my family had great respect for the Russians; they had allowed me to study the language for that reason and they had fled from German-occupied Poland in order to seek protection from the Soviet authorities. To my dismay, the colonel turned away from me.

'You are lying. Your story is a total fabrication put together in case you were captured.'

They confiscated my trouser belt and bootlaces. Clutching at the waistband of my trousers to keep them up, I continued to plead with the colonel. But he was now beginning to get bored. Standing up again, he ordered me to put my hands on my head. My trousers automatically fell down around my ankles. This sight was greeted with derision by the soldiers whilst I stood in silent embarrassment.

Leaning over the table, the colonel brought his face close to mine. His pungent tobacco breath made me wince as he bawled me out.

'I'm not as stupid as you seem to think. You'd better confess since it will be easier for both of us. Now, tell me why you violated the border. Why do you pretend to be a Pole when you have no Polish identity card? The reason is that you're a German! You think we are simple and ignorant but you're wrong. We can easily outwit you.'

I remained silent. Turning to the soldiers he said, 'Take him to the cellars. I'll speak to him again when I have more time. We'll have a special interrogation to make him "sing his song".'

Clutching my trousers at the waistband, with the bayonet almost piercing my skin, I tried to negotiate the steps to the cellar without losing my boots. The cellar door was heavily barred and padlocked. The smell outside the room was fetid, but it was bliss compared to the stench that greeted me when the door swung open. Before I had time to become aware of my surroundings, a rifle butt hit me between the shoulder blades and I was sent sprawling into the dirty, stinking darkness.

As my eyes began to grow accustomed to the dark, I saw that there were no windows and no ventilation. The floor was of earth. Covering my nose and mouth with the remnants of my shirt, I realised that the unbearable smell was caused by piles of human excrement, vomit and urine which practically covered the entire floor. In a corner I could make out what appeared to be coal. Since it was the cleanest part of the room, I propped myself up against the wall there and began to think. My thoughts wandered back to the Jesuits and I started to convince myself that this was God's punishment for my not following the Church. There seemed to be no way out. I was doomed to die in this hell-hole. I attempted to meditate, trying to release my soul from my exhausted body, and I prayed for deliverance. My body relaxed with the effort of meditation and I fell into an uncomfortable, restless sleep.

Cramp and cold woke me but the stench soon reminded me of my surroundings. Looking up as I stretched my limbs, I was aware of a small beam of light in the ceiling. Gathering the coal into a pile, I clambered up nearer the light. A huge iron cover hid the entrance to the coal shute. Holding it open about an inch, I managed to wedge a piece of coal between the base and the cover. With relief I filled my lungs with fresh, cold October air. The new ventilation occasionally wafted cold air into the cellar temporarily dispersing the smell. Occasionally I would stand on the coal, pressing my nose and mouth to the gap.

Nevertheless my spirit was broken; I spent my lonely hours either talking to God, actually holding a conversation with him as if he were in the room – was I on the verge of insanity? – or in a fitful sleep. It was during one of these bouts of sleep that I became aware of the echoing sound of the key turning in the lock and then voices. Opening my eyes I could see the silhouettes of eight people but it was obvious that they had not seen me. Having spent two nights sleeping among the coal, I was filthy and blended into the background. As their eyes became accustomed to the darkness they saw me, making a semi-circle round me, presuming I was a corpse. I moved and they drew back, startled, but soon approached me again.

They too had been caught by the patrol, arrested and inter-rogated and thrown in the cellar apparently because the makeshift prison was full. Midway through our conversation, a soldier opened the door and called my name, adding the words 'German spy'. I managed to crawl to the door, climbing the stairs with great difficulty, and was swept along the corridor by two soldiers and deposited in the interrogation room. A fourth person had joined my earlier interrogators at the table, a slim man with rather wild penetrating eyes, dressed in civilian clothes. The interrogation was conducted by him. In a calm, quiet voice he asked me my name, where I lived and, if I was a Pole, why I possessed a German passport.

I begged him for a cup of water since my throat was parched and I had difficulty speaking. I asked him if he was aware that I had been starved for three days and told him about the conditions in the cellar, pointing to my dirty boots and tattered clothing, adding that I had not expected such conditions in Russia. He looked questioningly at the colonel who in turn glared at me.

'I will see to it,' he muttered, as a soldier placed a cup of water in front of me. Slowly I drank, choking on the first two mouthfuls, letting the water swill round my mouth and down my throat. Only when I had finished every drop did I replace my cup. I then explained that I did not hold a German passport, that what I had was a German ID card which enabled me to travel around German-occupied Poland. He ordered me to translate the documents for him. This I did. He seemed more intelligent than his companions and, as I translated, I had a glimmer of hope that perhaps he would believe my story. He asked me why I could speak so many languages and I told him I had excelled in them at the Jesuit college. I tried to steer his questioning towards my family but he would not discuss them.

'We will talk about your family later. I must have the truth first. Shall we try again?'

I replied in a controlled voice, trying to match his mood.

'I was born in Poland, my father is a Pole, my mother is Austrian. I have never set foot in Germany. I do not know any Germans. I have no desire to know any Germans. This whole thing is a complete farce.'

I think he knew that I was telling the truth and he did not like it. His tone of voice changed.

'That is enough. Now, let's have the truth, you bloody German swine! If you don't confess I shall have to teach you a lesson. Are you aware that I have the authority to shoot you?' He took his gun out of its holster and placed it on the table in front of us.

'The laws seem to have changed since the Occupation,' I replied. 'Why don't you shoot me? It's better than starving to death in your stinking cellar.'

The interrogation started again, the questions coming fast and furious. Where were my headquarters? Who did I report back to? How many more spies had infiltrated the east? My answer remained the same: I had escaped from German-occupied territory and I was searching for my family, hoping to obtain Soviet cooperation. Anger made his voice tremble as he thumped the table repeatedly, screaming for the truth and threatening to shoot.

The questions were repeated time after time. I remained calm, knowing that if I started to lose my temper I would risk being shot. My interrogator kept touching his gun as he fired questions at me but my answers remained the same.

As suddenly as the questioning had started, it stopped. New tactics were introduced. The colonel turned to his companions.

'It's mealtime, gentlemen; I've ordered our dinner to be served in here.'

I was pushed into a corner, told to put my hands on my head and watch the four men eat.

They acted as if they were sitting in a restaurant, totally ignoring me, laughing and joking, drinking and eating, and smoking their cigarettes after the meal.

'Now then, my friend,' again the change of attitude in his voice, 'your meal is waiting. Just answer our few simple questions truthfully.'

A repetition of the questions followed and I gave the same answers, asking them this time to seek out my brothers in Poland to verify my story. I added, somewhat daringly, that I had crossed the border for freedom, not to be thrown into prison. Still he shouted until I thought my head would burst. Eventually the colonel intervened and in a superior tone of voice said:

'You've had your chance and your confession is not forthcoming. We could shoot you but then we'd have a dead German spy on our hands. That's not practical so we will see if the Lubianka prison in Moscow will open your mouth. Take him to the cellar!'

The soldiers manhandled me out of the room, dragging my tired body down the steps into the corridor, throwing me against the wall whilst they unlocked the door. Then, they pushed me back into the filthy cellar. I had been in the interrogation room for eight hours and my new companions presumed I had gone to my death. I told them what had happened. One of the Jews had dealt with Soviet officialdom and he explained the system. Catching a spy was rewarded with medals and the chance of promotion. Proof could easily be fabricated in their perverted system and most suspects were proved to be spies whether they were or not. Failure to show proof would result in loss of reputation. Obviously the young Russian interrogator had visions of grandeur and an extra medal pinned to his chest. He was not going to give in and there was nothing I could do to get out of his clutches.

At any rate, the colonel kept his word about the food and water. The following morning the door was unlocked and a bucket of boiling water was brought into the cellar. Nine pieces of bread and nine herrings followed. The guard stood in the doorway issuing his orders. When we had finished the water we were to use the bucket to urinate in. It was my responsibility as a German spy, he said, to empty the bucket every morning. I ate slowly, my stomach not used to food. I cupped my hands and drank the still-warm water. It tasted like nectar.

A daily ritual started. In the early morning the guard would unlock the door and I would take the bucket of urine to the toilet under the guard's supervision, wash the bucket and wait for it to be filled with boiling water. I was then given nine pieces of bread and nine herrings, which was our entire food for the day. The guard became friendly during these daily jaunts. Occasionally he let me use the toilet whilst I waited for the boiling water. Maybe he was hoping I would confide in me. In the event it was he who confided in me. He had heard that we were to be transported away from this border area. When I asked him where, he just shrugged his shoulders and muttered, 'Siberia?'

I told my cellmates. We all agreed that anywhere would be better than this stinking hell-hole. But the journey was over before it started for two of the group. Taken ill suddenly, they vomited continually, the yellow bile mixed with blood. I thought it was cholera and reported my fears to the guard. The following morning the near-dead Jews were removed. That night we comforted the sons of the dead men, praying for their souls. At least *their* sufferings had come to an end.

# Chapter Eight

## *The Journey*

Having heard rumours of our impending journey, we became impatient. Each day seemed interminable. We discussed plans for escaping but the only possible exit was via the coal chute and we knew that a 24-hour guard patrolled close by. It was late afternoon when they finally came for us, the sound of the key in the lock filling us with expectation.

Four Red Army soldiers entered the cellar, recoiling immediately when the stench hit them. Trying not to breathe, they issued their orders and we were herded out of the cellar into the open air. Twenty other people, obviously from the prison, were waiting outside the headquarters, among them the Jews with whom I had shared the boat on that fateful night. We were formed into a column, a soldier at each corner and ordered to 'Poganiaj'.

My lungs began to fill with the fresh clean air and the cold wind stung my eyes, making them water. We were all in a similar condition, tired, hungry, filthy and sick since conditions had not been much better in the makeshift prison. For an hour we marched, the guards treating us like animals, hurling abuse at us as they tried to hurry us to our 'collection point'. This turned out to be a disused stable at the side of the railway track. The windows had been boarded up so that only the occasional gleams of sunlight penetrated the room. Iron bars were secured on the outside of the boards. The floor was of bare cobblestones and I couldn't resist making the comment that if we had been horses at least we would have had some straw. We were ordered into three stalls, ten or more prisoners being squeezed into a stall big enough for one horse. This was to be our home for as long as it took the other prisoners to arrive. Once my eyes grew accustomed to the dark, I could see other stalls, all completely full, each person trying to get some sleep in the cramped conditions.

The cattle train was already waiting for its human cargo, but we were told we could not be loaded until sufficient prisoners had arrived to fill all the wagons. The soldiers' intention was to fill each truck with thirty to forty people in a space designed to carry approximately eight cows, travelling comfortably. The rationale behind the cramming in of bodies was that, sooner or later, many, perhaps most, of the prisoners would perish owing to the strenuous physical pressures in the camps, in particular the hunger and cold of the Siberian winter. By keeping them under these conditions on the trains, the weakest would expire before they reached the camps, thus making room for the stronger prisoners. Millions of Poles, Ukrainians, Estonians, Latvians and Lithuanians, not to mention Russians, lost their lives in this way during Stalin's rule.

Prisoners continued to arrive all through the night and by morning I estimated that roughly 800 people were in the cramped barn. At first light we were confronted by a squad of Red Army soldiers. These were the 'segregators' who passed among us, placing us in groups. Prisoners who had confessed to their crimes, most of them innocent but unable to withstand the rigours of interrogation, were grouped in batches of thirty to forty. The political prisoners and those who had not confessed to any crime, myself included, were put into groups of twenty. Obviously, given more room, we were expected to survive the journey to Moscow whilst the common prisoners, having confessed, had already sealed their fate. If they survived the overcrowding, they would not survive the cold, stark, Siberian forests. The old, infirm and disabled were segregated into a corner of the barn whereupon they were ordered to wait for 'special treatment'.

The guards began to load the human cargo, starting with the groups of common prisoners. As in the barn, the windows in the trucks were heavily boarded and barred. In the centre of the floor of each truck was a large hole to enable the truck to be cleared of cattle dung. Over the hole had been placed an iron plate with smaller holes bored into it. This provided us with our only form of sanitation.

The next group to board were the political prisoners, or spies, who had confessed or had been found guilty by the Soviet authorities. They too were journeying to the Siberian labour camps, their fate sealed by their confessions, their punishment a minimum of ten years in the camp. In these camps, in places like Pechora, Vorkuta and Kolyma, hardly anyone survived for more than five years. A ten-year sentence was equivalent to a death penalty. Since the Communists did not want their prison tactics revealed to the world, they made sure that no one came out of those camps alive.

It was while we were waiting to board the train that a huge army lorry arrived. I still remember it vividly. The thirty or more 'rejects' were ushered out of the barn and loaded into the lorry. Those that could not climb of their own accord were literally picked up and thrown in by the soldiers as they chanted 'Fine Polish soap, fine Polish soap'. When the last person had been manhandled into the back, a heavy tarpaulin was thrown over them and fastened down with strong rope. The lorry drove away. It was an incident that still lives in my memory. The soldiers were sent at regular intervals to pick up these poor unfortunate people and to end their lives. The words 'fine Polish soap' haunted my dreams and thoughts for many years.

I was still watching, horror-stricken, when I realised we were the next to be boarded. We were the prisoners heading for the Lubianka prison, the stubborn ones who would not confess. We knew what awaited us: interrogation, torture, shootings in cold blood. A confession or a guilty verdict would mean a Siberian labour camp for the rest of our lives.

Twenty of us were manhandled into the truck. It was cramped but did not smell as bad as the cellar. When the door was closed and bolted we were thrust into darkness. We each tried to claim a little bit of space but there was no light or ventilation and very little room. I thought about the other trucks with thirty or forty people inside and shuddered.

The train began its slow, laborious journey. With my back pressed against the side of the truck, I managed to slide into a sitting position and stretched my legs out in front of me. Beside me sat a young soldier roughly the same age as me, named Tadek. By taking it in turns to lean on one another, we managed to catch a few hours' sleep. Ventilation was the biggest problem. The prisoners in the centre of the truck slept curled up in a ball, their noses pressed to the bore-holes. This hindered the ventilation for the rest of us and caused heated arguments. It was not until one of our party died of a heart attack owing to lack of oxygen that they agreed to move and use the bore-holes for their original purpose. Eventually, fearing that we might all die of the same plight, we managed to prise off a small piece of the boarding, enabling more air to circulate.

The ritual that was to last for almost two months began. Each morning the train would stop, each truck was opened and the dead were dragged out feet first and deposited in the mortuary truck at the end of the train. We had been issued with two buckets per truck, one for water, the other for our daily supply of herrings and bread. On the order 'Prepare buckets!' we had to hold them at arm's length outside the truck in order to have them filled. If, for any reason, they were not forthcoming, we would go hungry and thirsty for that day. At each large station, provisions and water were taken on board. These were kept in the specially-prepared carriages with full home comforts that housed the soldiers and members of the NKVD. Needless to say, they were spared the overcrowding and the absence of sanitation which we experienced. While supplies were being taken on board, the mortuary truck was uncoupled and replaced by an empty truck.

The journey was extremely tedious. Some mornings we would stop for our daily rituals only to find we had been shunted into a siding to give priority to a passing goods or passenger train. Whole days of travel were lost in this way. The guards' priority was security. Anyone attempting to escape was shot and we cringed every time we heard the echo of a single gunshot nearby.

Tadek became a good friend. He had been arrested 100 yards from the border of German-occupied Poland. The new frontier between Germany and the Soviet Union divided him from his girlfriend, she being in the German part and he in the Soviet. Twice a week he would pit his wits against the authorities and sneak across the border to spend a few precious hours with the girl he hoped to marry. His luck eventually ran out one night on his return. Lone trespassers were usually shot on sight but he was lucky. He surrendered, put his hands on his head and waited for the bullet to pierce his chest but it did not come. Instead he was taken prisoner and treated in much the same way as me. Hence his long journey to the Lubianka.

Tadek was very clever and not afraid to risk his life. He got away with things on that terrible journey that most people would have been shot for. During one stopping period, whilst waiting for the guard to fill our bucket, he jumped out of the truck, scooped up the fresh white snow and distributed it among our group before the provisions soldier reached our truck. The virgin snow tasted like nectar compared with our usual drinking water, which was sometimes mixed with oil from the locomotive.

Though living with the knowledge that he would probably never see the girl he loved again, Tadek managed to keep our spirits up during the journey. He told jokes about the Russians and orga- nised silly guessing games to keep our brains from stagnating totally. He cajoled those of the group who were ready to 'end it all' and prophesied better things to come. We all knew he was dreaming, but his light-hearted approach to life helped us to keep our sanity and saved many from sinking deeply into depres- sion.

It was late December when rumours began to circulate that we had reached Moscow. We halted in a siding. Outside, the snow was knee-deep and through the hole in the boards we could just make out a station and what appeared to be a 'centre of activity'. When the door of the truck opened the icy blast of the blizzard made us recoil into the shelter of the truck. Confronting us, clothed in huge fur overcoats, medals pinned on their lapels, stood three members of the NKVD.

One of the men, a captain judging from the three stars on his lapel, addressed us. He had a list of names and began his roll call. Each person, when his name was called, stepped forward and was ordered to sit in the snow either to the right or to the left. Occasionally the name of a dead person was called. On hearing the word 'deceased' from one of the soldiers, the name was struck off the list and the person's papers were destroyed. My name was called and I stepped forward. I was ordered to the left. Tadek squeezed my hand and wished me good luck. When his name was called, he was ordered to the right. We looked across at each other knowing that we would never meet again.

We on the left, fifteen in all, were to go to the Lubianka for further interrogation under Article 58, for alleged spying and other counter-revolutionary activities. We were ordered to 'poganiaj' through the knee-deep snow to the black high-sided lorry waiting to take us to the dreaded prison.

# Chapter Nine

## *The Lubianka*

The cold was intense and soon ice began to form on our clothes as the lorry ploughed its way through the deep snow. During the hour-long journey we huddled together for extra warmth, sheltering as best we could in the corner of the lorry, the canvas shielding us from the snow but providing no warmth. Eventually we came to a halt. We heard the sound of heavy gates opening and then closing after us as the lorry drove through. The lorry stopped again. I presumed we'd arrived at the dreaded Lubianka, the prison where, rumour had it, if you saw the inside you would not live to describe it.

The guards ordered us out of the lorry. As our eyes grew accustomed to the light and the brightness of the snow we saw, looming up in front of us, a huge six-storey building complete with ominous observation towers. Taking in this oppressive scene, I felt terrified of what was in store.

We were split into two groups and taken into separate rooms. Our room was small, with crude wooden benches placed against the walls. The floor was made of rough concrete with a large drainage trough running through the middle.

'Remove all your clothes for the de-lousing process.' The guard's voice echoed across the room. I cringed, daring to look at my companions who, like robots, were already removing their garments. I began to strip, not happy with the situation but knowing that I stood no chance against the guards. When the door opened I was shocked to see two masculine-looking, overweight women lumbering into the room carrying two buckets of pungent water and a number of cloths. It was obvious that neither had ever won a beauty competition.

One by one we were approached and told to wash ourselves with the de-lousing fluid paying close attention to our hair and genital areas. We were then passed on to the second woman who had the task of shaving us. The women spoke to each other as they performed their duties. It was obvious that they regarded us with contempt as they ridiculed our lean, hungry frames whilst shaving our most private parts. When they had finished we were completely hairless, even the hair on our chests and buttocks had been removed by the razors, which we were not allowed to touch lest we go berserk and try to attack the women. After shaving we were ordered to wash once more in the repulsive liquid, which stung our now hairless bodies.

Next we were ushered into a cubicle adjoining the room where an ice-cold shower numbed our bodies but stopped the stinging sensation. Our clothes, which also had to be deloused, were bundled together. We were assured they would be returned to us on our release. We were each given a fresh bundle of clothing. I had a shirt, three sizes too large, a pair of prison trousers, threadbare at the knees and a pair of badly worn shoes without laces. We looked a motley crew in our 'new' clothes as we were taken down to the cells and distributed wherever there was a vacant bed.

I was taken to one of the larger cells which contained six pairs of bunk beds, twelve prisoners, a table and buckets for our daily needs. An air of despondency hung over the cell and the inmates seemed very subdued. Finally the man in the bunk opposite spoke.

'You must be exhausted my friend. Have some of this bread and water.' I accepted gratefully. 'We are very sad today. The man who occupied your bed, in fact the man whose bread you have just eaten, was taken away today to be executed. He was a good man. Many of the prisoners here are peasants. They don't comprehend what is happening to them, the implication of being in this prison. I can see you are intelligent my friend. He was intelligent. That's why they shot him.'

I commiserated with them, and the ice was broken. I learned that food and drink were brought three times a day, that the days were long and boring but that with the extra food and extra rest I would soon regain some of my former strength. They advised me to save my strength in order to survive the ordeal of interrogation. I rested on my hard wooden bed. I was so cold and weak that the prospect of death no longer daunted me. I slept well, in fact this was the first time I had actually slept on a bed for three months. The food was quite delicious after my diet of herrings and bread and I felt my strength returning. Conversation between the prisoners was infrequent. Sometimes the guards would take one of our cellmates for interrogation and we would take bets on whether or not we would see him again.

My friend was intelligent and a good conversationalist. He told me his life story. I was taken aback to learn that he was an orthodox priest who had been arrested in his home town, accused of teaching religion to the local children. He was awaiting his fate, knowing he had no chance of proving his innocence. He began to quiz me about my life. At first I was non-committal since my trust in my fellow human beings was diminishing fast, but after a few days I began to unwind and slowly started to relate my story. He listened intently and when I had finished he looked at me in amazement.

'Like most of us you are innocent,' he said. 'I know how the Soviet Criminal Codes work. It makes no difference whether you are guilty or innocent, you will be charged under Article 58, paragraph 6, "Suspected Spying". You will then be interrogated by the NKVD who will force you to sign a 'voluntary' confession. It is at this point that you hold your fate balanced in the palm of your hand. You can sign the confession, but if you do you'll condemn yourself to execution. If that's what you decide, you can rest assured that I will absolve you from your sins and give you the final blessing, ensuring your journey to heaven. However, if you decide to sign the confession but to plead for leniency, your life will be spared, much to the satisfaction of the authorities. They will then

51

send you off to one of their labour camps where you will provide them with unpaid labour for the rest of your short life. When my time comes, I know which course I will take.'

He touched me and I felt a feeling of peace flow through his fingertips. The Jesuits too had this gift of transferring peace and tranquillity.

'One more thing, don't object to being called a German. Ten times as many Poles and Russians as Germans are shot, so you probably have a better chance of surviving than the rest of us.'

I relaxed, my mind reviewing the options open to me and secretly admiring the man who had decided to die for his religion and his God.

I now had time to find out about the Lubianka. Thousands of prisoners passed through it on their way either to concentration camps or sudden death. There were almost as many interrogation rooms as there were cells. These rooms were in constant use. I found out many things about the prison from the prisoners themselves, who passed on their own experiences and the experiences of the ex-prisoners who had already departed for the labour camps or been executed. I was surprised to hear that they had women interrogators and that they were even more sadistic than the men. After my experiences in the de-lousing room I was prepared to believe that half a dozen amazons in a room would be enough to grind any man into a shivering wreck.

'Natasha' was a name to conjure up terror among the inmates. Anyone having been interrogated by Natasha bore the scars for life. She was known as the 'Angel of Death'; an extremely beautiful woman with a heart of stone.

My first experience of Natasha's work came a few days later when one of our cell-mates, a Russian army officer sentenced for offending the army 'Politrook', was taken away for interrogation. He was away for four hours and when he was brought back to the cell he was unconscious, on the verge of death. We carried him to his bunk. His body was covered in sweat and his clothes were wet and sticky. We stripped him in order to sponge his body, unprepared for the shock that awaited us. The sticky substance was blood. On removing his trousers, we recoiled in horror at the blood pouring out of a hole where his testicles should have been. The prisoners spoke in whispers, totally shocked and unable to touch the poor unfortunate man.

It was the priest who took control of the situation, placing his hand on the young soldier and absolving him of his sins. We joined in the prayers for his salvation. Gently bathing the soldier's forehead, the priest spoke to us in a calm, hushed voice. What we had seen confirmed the truth of the rumours about Natasha; that if she were unable to obtain a confession, she had her victim spread-eagled on a table and then squeezed and twisted his genitals with a pair of cobbler's tongs until a confession was forthcoming. If the prisoner still did not confess, she would rip the poor man's testicles from his body and he would be taken back to his cell to die as a warning to his cell-mates.

The unconscious man stirred, his eyes opened and in a rasping vote he strained:

'She used the cobbler's tongs, the bastard bitch! But I didn't confess.' With the effort of speaking, he lost consciousness once more and died ten minutes later.

My strength was beginning to return. I realised that to survive interrogation I would have to be fit and so, every morning on rising, I did press-ups on the rough concrete floor. Other prisoners soon realised that this was a good idea and we would take it in turns to exercise before the guard came with our breakfast.

I had been in the Lubianka for four weeks when I finally received my order to 'poganiaj'. My time had come. The two Red Army soldiers standing in the doorway called out my name, adding the words 'German spy'. All eyes turned on me. Not a word was spoken. I was sandwiched between the two soldiers and escorted out of the cell.

Gritting my teeth, I was determined to tell the truth. I still could not believe that one human being could ill-treat another simply for telling the truth. I should have known better. How many times had

I seen my fellow cell-mates return with swollen faces, teeth missing, torn fingernails and badly bruised bodies!

I congratulated myself on being prepared both mentally and physically as I entered the interrogation room. I digested my environment; the walls were padded, obviously to provide sound-proofing; a long, strong table and two chairs were the only furniture in the room; facing me on the wall hung a picture of Stalin and above his head were two red Soviet flags, the golden hammer and sickle embossed on them standing out and almost intimidating me. A packet of cigarettes, matches and a cardboard file were the only articles on the table. One soldier remained with me, standing silently staring into space. Ten minutes of sheer panic followed. I looked first at the table, then at the flags, then I stared into Stalin's eyes, the portrait almost coming alive under my stare. Finally I let my eyes drop to the newly-scrubbed floor, searching for dark patches of discoloured concrete.

Suddenly the soldier stood to attention. The door opened and a tall, middle-aged man wearing the three stars of a captain and carrying a large Russian revolver in his holster entered. He smiled at me warmly, giving the impression that I was his long-lost friend.

'*Zdrastuite?*' (How do you do?)

He sat down, methodically picked up the cigarette packet, took one for himself and offered me one, lighting my cigarette first like a perfect gentleman. He then opened the file.

I had not tasted a cigarette for six months and I swallowed heavily on the smoke, content to let him peruse my file whilst I enjoyed this luxury. He finished his cigarette, clasping his hands in front of him on the table.

'What is your name?'

I answered.

'Can you speak the Russian language?' he asked.

I nodded.

'Good, good. I am your friend here and I would like you to read this report. If you agree with it please sign your name. I'm sure you would like to remain my friend since I can protect you from some of my colleagues who, I might add, are very bloodthirsty. However, I can only help you if you agree to co-operate.'

He passed me the report. It listed a number of fictitious spying activities, ending with a description of my capture on the German/Russian border. It noted that a German passport had been seized on my arrest and that my failure to co-operate with the authorities had shown proof of my guilt. When I had finished reading this nonsense, I placed the report on the table.

'This is a total fabrication. I cannot sign anything that is not the truth.'

'That is entirely up to you, my friend. Remember, the evidence produced in this file is enough to prove your guilt. You'll receive a death penalty. Surely it's better to confess and sign and then we can show you leniency and spare your life.'

I shook my head, refusing to be part of this.

'Please, listen to me,' I begged him. 'I can convince you of my innocence. I escaped from German-occupied territory after serving in the Polish army fighting the Germans. I crossed the border in search of my parents who had escaped the German occupation. In all honesty I came seeking your protection as they did before me.'

He picked up his papers, a grim expression on his face.

'So, you insist that the people responsible for this report are liars, including Colonel Korylov, a Russian hero who possesses Stalin's highest order? He signed this report! Surely you don't think I'm stupid enough to accuse the colonel of lying?'

He pushed the papers back towards me, pointing to his pen. I shook my head.

'I cannot sign my name confessing to crimes I have not committed. I am ready to die for my principles.'

His voice changed, all traces of friendliness gone.

'We shall see, we shall see. I shall send for you again tonight when you have had time to think about the implications.'

The second guard unlocked the door and I was escorted back to my cell.

I waited anxiously for my recall but my name was not called that night. Instead a Ukrainian soldier was called. Since he did not return we assumed he had been shot. Every night at about seven o'clock we heard the rattling of the machine-guns in the yard, then deathly silence. If you had not been sent for by seven o'clock, you knew you would live to see another day. I was despondent, blaming myself for his death. I should have been executed; why had they taken him?

The priest, knowing my turmoil, tried to explain.

'He was ready for death. He's been waiting since his last interrogation. Once they have sentenced you to death they do not take you straight away but keep you waiting, to prolong your agony. I absolved him of sins many weeks ago. His soul is no longer tormented. He is at rest.'

Incredibly it was six weeks before my name was called again. This time there was no friendliness, no offering of cigarettes, just three stern-faced men, the captain among them, seated in front of the watchful eye of Stalin. It was the captain who spoke.

'I have re-read your papers. All the evidence points to your guilt. We want to gain your co-operation so we have made contact with your family, your Polish father, your German mother, your brothers and sisters. They are all in our care. In punishment for your spying activities, they have been sent to labour camps, provided they survive the journey.'

He went on: 'The only punishment in the Soviet Union for any counter-revolutionary activities is death by a bullet through the head. However, because your family are paying for your crimes, we will give you a choice once again. If you sign this newly-prepared document accusing you of "suspected spying" we will spare you. Otherwise you will be shot right here in this room.'

I banged my fist down on the hard table.

'Shoot me! What are you waiting for? You know the evidence is fabricated. And I don't believe that my family is in your "care".'

I lunged forward. While one of the guards restrained me, the captain drew his revolver and pointed it at my head. I closed my eyes. I then heard a shot and felt something heavy strike my neck and automatically I lost consciousness. How long I remained unconscious I do not know. I remember the water reviving me and, opening my eyes, I saw the soldier standing over me with the empty bucket. My body and head ached – I had obviously been kicked several times – but I was surprised to be alive. I was aware of the captain shouting.

'Death is too good for you, "German spy"! If you won't confess you must suffer! When we have finished with you maybe a bullet through your brain will be welcome relief!'

The soldiers came forward, kicking me around the room like a football. I was too weak to resist and there was no escaping the heavy jackboots. I thought earlier I had regained my strength but I was proved wrong. As I slipped quietly into oblivion I remember thinking that at least I had been spared Natasha and her cobbler's tongs.

Some time during the night the beating stopped. The soldiers were gone and I was still huddled upon the bare concrete floor. I heard a movement and through my swollen eyes I could see the silhouette of the captain standing over me. I muttered to him that I would sign his paper but on condition that they shot me as soon as I had signed. He smiled. He had won, and soon another medal would be coming his way. He placed the pen in my hand and I signed my death warrant.

I closed my eyes and waited in vain for the shot that would put me out of my misery. Instead two guards entered the room and since I was unable to stand they picked me up bodily and carried me to a different cell, where I would have to wait until they received the authority to shoot me. I immediately slipped into unconsciousness which brought temporary relief for my aching body. When I finally awoke I was surprised to see that I shared the cell with about eighteen other prisoners. Someone offered me a drink and I forced the mug between my bruised lips.

This cell faced onto the execution yard and that night we got a preview of what could shortly be our fate. At seven o'clock, twenty naked prisoners with hands on heads were herded into the yard and lined up against the concrete wall. The soldiers, each carrying a machine-gun, faced them. We heard the voice of the corporal ordering them to shoot. A few short blasts of machine-gun fire followed. Blood from the naked bodies of the victims coloured the wall and the ground beneath them was red as the Soviet flag. The soldiers then proceeded to prod the bodies for any sign of life. Any sign of movement was met with a bayonet stab right through the heart.

When all signs of life had gone, the lorry arrived, the human carcasses were thrown into the back and a tarpaulin was thrown over them and secured. They were taken away to be disposed of.

As soon as the lorry had gone, the soldiers brought in water and brushes, swilling the still-warm blood into the gutters, making the yard spotlessly clean in readiness for the next day's victims. These executions were carried out daily in the Lubianka whilst Stalin was in power.

The following morning we were given a good breakfast, which was a bad sign. My mouth was swollen and I could hardly eat but now that I had survived their beatings I was not sure that I wanted to die. After breakfast six soldiers arrived. As I levered my battered body into a standing position, I thought this was the end. Formed into twos we were taken across the execution yard and into a damp room which was the shower room. We were ordered to strip and shower. As I stood under the cold shower inspecting my bruised body, the coldness numbed the pain and revived my sagging spirits. Yesterday I had wanted to die but now I wanted to live.

Dressed in our prison rags, we followed the soldiers into the main building where we awaited our fate. The prisoners were called according to the seriousness of their crimes. Several of us, myself included, were awaiting the death penalty. I waited and waited, expecting to be one of the first to be called but when my name was finally shouted there were only three of us remaining. Entering the room, I saw it was much the same as the interrogation room but without the padding on the wall. Instead of a picture of

Stalin there was a statue, but the two red flags were still in evidence, crossed on the wall above his head.

The man behind the table looked sombre in his dark clothing. He was grey-haired and wore a pair of thick-lensed glasses. 'My friend' the captain stood on his right, a younger man on his left, a huge bundle of files spread out in front of him. I was ordered to attention, feet together, arms at my side. The younger man asked me my name and handed the appropriate file to the prosecutor, who started to read out the charges against me: 'That on such and such a date in the town of Przemysl I had been arrested in the Russian Protectorate territory by the Russian hero, Army Colonel Korylov, with the help of his distinguished army patrol. Being in possession of a German passport, I was accused of espionage duties . . .' etc. His voice droned on, but finally, he said:

'For espionage as for any counter-revolutionary behaviour, the only punishment in the Soviet Union is death.'

The captain interrupted him and a whispered conversation took place. With an evil smile on his face, the captain turned to me.

'I understand you confessed to all your crimes and so we can offer you leniency. Your sentence is therefore reduced to ten years' hard labour in a specially designed camp in Siberia. However, owing to the gravity of this case, I am recommending that when your ten years' servitude is over you will remain in exile in northern Siberia for the rest of your miserable life.'

My papers were signed and I was returned to my first cell to wait for transport to the 'deportation camp'. My cellmates were glad to see me. I held up ten fingers to signify I had got ten years. They were relieved. As I rested my weary body on my bunk I hoped that with God's help I would survive.

# Chapter Ten

# *The Journey to Pechora Lager*

Back in the company of my friends, I waited a week before I heard the familiar sound of the guards unlocking the cell doors and shouting out the names of the prisoners for the deportation centre. Eventually I heard my name called. After a sad leave-taking from my cellmates, I left the prison and was marched along with twenty others to join thousands of prisoners in the Moscow 'slave trading centre'. The entire area in which we were confined resembled a huge cattle market, with the prisoners separated into various pens or sections.

There were three main categories of prisoners, political, non-political and religious; these were further divided into 'year sections', i.e. prisoners with ten-, fifteen- or twenty-five-year sentences. Each prisoner was placed in the appropriate section depending on his sentence. I was in the political section, ten-year category.

The centre was no less than a major commercial undertaking. Hundreds of soldiers guarded the various groups, while representatives from various labour camps strolled between the sections looking for manpower, selecting the strongest and bartering all the while with the NKVD officers in charge. The latter were only too eager to get the prisoners off their hands in order to fulfil their 'output' targets set by government commissars. Some of the 'buyers' insisted on examining the prisoners as if they were working horses, feeling their muscles, checking their teeth, and generally looking for any defects that might affect the length of their working life. This was a sham; it was obvious just by looking at us that most of us were thin, under-nourished and out of condition. Examination like this only added to our feelings of degradation.

The older, more mature prisoners and those with eye and hearing problems were picked for the salt and coal mines where their expectation of life was only three to four years. Their fate was unremitting labour underground, without a glimpse of daylight. They would come to the surface only after death, when their wasted bodies would be brought up for burial in a communal grave.

Those not selected for the mines were sent to work building railways, the nearest camps for this work being in Kotlas en route to Vorkuta. The railway journey to these camps was not as arduous and the older prisoners had a better chance of reaching them. But the work was extremely rigorous and out of many thousands of prisoners, only a small number survived. Rumour had it that more slaves died constructing this endless iron road than there were wooden railway sleepers under the track.

But the largest contingent of 'buyers' came from the Pechora Forestry Commission. The extreme winter of 1939–40 had taken its toll of prisoners working in the huge forests along the Pechora river. Frostbite and malnutrition during those gruelling winter months had decimated the forest gangs and their numbers had to be made up. The 'buyers' knew what they were looking for, hurrying to each section to select young prisoners who appeared reasonably strong and agile. Those chosen were whisked away to be officially stamped with a large green letter 'L', which stood for the 'Lespromcos' administration. I was one of 300 prisoners chosen for this work. But first we had to wait for the cattle trucks to take us on our horrible journey north to Pechora Camp. These trucks arrived daily, and were loaded with their human cargo for the return journey.

I had to wait four days for my turn to board. In addition to the 300 going to Pechora, there were prisoners going to various other camps. The conditions were the same as on our journey to Moscow, twenty-five to thirty men squashed into each truck, huddling together for comfort and warmth, and with the same rations of herring, bread and water. By now the winter weather had really taken a grip and the further north we travelled the colder it became.

Gorki was the first official stop. Peering through the barred window, I counted about fifty prisoners and a handful of guards standing knee-deep in the snow waiting for transportation to their camps. The next stop was Kirov. Here the train was emptied of all prisoners except those going to Pechora. We heard that those who disembarked at Kirov were going to Kotlas and from there northwards into the bitter cold of Vorkuta, on the Arctic Circle. The rest of us were despatched further east towards Perm. For the remainder of our journey, we were allowed to spread out in the empty trucks and get some sleep. At the time we did not realise how lucky we were.

Berezniki was the last stop on the line. The construction gangs had been struggling to make progress during the winter months and the death rate among the prisoners was extremely high. Much to the government's dissatisfaction, progress on the line was behind schedule. On the journey the guards constantly drilled into us that Stalin's programme had to be completed. Since failure would be blamed on the soldiers and NKVD officials, we knew they'd be ruthless in forcing us to reach our output targets.

Little did we know, on our arrival at Berezniki, that ahead of us lay a journey of 280 miles which had to be covered on foot. The only communication with the north otherwise was by horse and sledge. The unloading of the train was a slow process, since each prisoner had to be shackled to another to minimise the chances of escape, as there were only three guards to each fifty prisoners. The guards themselves had the privilege of riding on a long low sledge pulled by a strong Siberian horse. We trudged behind it. I was thankful that my partner was young and quite agile since we could keep in step more easily and help each other through the snowdrifts.

Advanced parties of prisoners had pioneered the journey,

building barracks at twenty-mile intervals to accommodate those who came after. Hence we had a long trek before reaching our next food, water and shelter. That first stage left us tired, numb with cold and hungry. The sight of the stark wooden barracks elated us and the smell of food made love to our nostrils. We were each given a bowl of gruel consisting of boiled fish heads, cabbage and potatoes, not very appetising but the warmth compensated for the taste, and we ate heartily. A cup of boiling water finished the meal. We moved the hot cup up and down our frozen legs and feet to get some feeling back. After this the guards announced we'd have to be up at dawn, when we'd be given some food and water ready for the next stage of the journey.

Since we were still shackled together sleep did not come easily, but the guards, despite requests, refused to take the risk of unshackling us. Daylight came all too soon. As we set off again, the guards spurred us on with promises of warm food and I must admit that the very thought of it made our steps quicken. Answering the call of nature was an embarrassment since the shackles were never unfastened and there was no privacy. Some prisoners preferred not to stop and soon began to stink of urine, which froze onto their clothing almost instantaneously. This made their clothes rigid and uncomfortable and as a result, their thighs and legs quickly turned sore.

There were three stops between Berezniki and Krasnovishersk but the journey was not without its casualties, ten prisoners dying during the first eighty miles. Many more fell victim before we reached the Pechora river. As we approached Krasnovishersk we were in a cold, hungry, weak and stinking condition. Relief flooded over us when the settlement appeared over the horizon. To my surprise the horses were reined to a standstill and the guards moved among us unlocking our padlocks and then removing them completely. We were allowed to walk the last half mile to the town minus our chains. It seemed that the guards didn't want the people in the settlement to think that they couldn't handle us, preferring to take the risk of attempted escape rather than face ridicule. It seemed not to occur to them that we were so weak and tired that we didn't have the energy to escape and survive.

The hot soup waiting for us was tastier than the gruel served at the barracks along the route, and we were each given an extra ration of bread. We were an unkempt, dirty bunch of travellers so it was not surprising when the officer in charge announced that we would have to be deloused. First our clothing was taken away and thrown into cleaning fluid. We were then taken into the shower room ten at a time, the water was turned on and for two whole minutes we were allowed the luxury of running water cleansing our bodies. We were provided with fresh clothing and our discarded clothes, after cleaning, were put away in readiness for the next batch of prisoners.

A three-day rest period was announced while we waited for a change of guard. The Russians who had brought us this far were not equipped to take us deep into the forests. Hereabouts the winters lasted for almost ten months and the snow rarely disappeared. Hence a hardy breed of guard was needed to escort us in these conditions. These were the 'Mongolian barbarians' who lived and worked in these Arctic conditions and were reputed to be sadistic and impatient.

We slept in huge bare rooms huddled together for warmth and companionship, three nights of comparative comfort and two meals a day helping to restore some of our lost energy. It was on the fourth day that 'all hell was let loose' when the Mongolians arrived and started to make vigorous preparations for the journey. We barely had time to drink our soup before they stormed into the room and ordered us to move into line. We were shackled together into six lines of about fifty prisoners each. Unlike the Russians, the Mongolians were proud to be in charge of so many prisoners chained together. As we walked through the centre of the settlement, they kicked and struck us for effect. Though the sledges and horses were available, they preferred to walk alongside the prisoners. Dressed in their furs they looked resplendent against the thin coats and worn-out shoes of their captives. They were not a race to be reasoned with, a fact that became more apparent as the journey went on.

Our first day passed relatively quickly since the snow was hard-packed and walking quite easy. Moreover, we were all refreshed after our short rest, so it was without much effort that we arrived at our first barrack stop having travelled twenty miles in the day. But the food was back to the staple diet of herring and bread and hot water once a day, and after the hot soup at Krasnovishersk it tasted revolting. We asked if our chains could be removed for the night to help us to sleep. We were given a short, sharp kick for our trouble and told to shut up.

First thing in the morning the Mongolians burst into the room. Before we could gather our wits they started dragging us to our feet ordering us outside into the freezing air. By now the conditions had deteriorated. The snow began to deepen as we veered off the beaten track and into the forests. It was difficult to keep your balance in these conditions and a line of prisoners would come to a halt as some of their number tumbled and fell in the deep snow. The guards became angry and began to drag the unfortunate prisoners to their feet, hurling abuse at them. Eventually one Ukrainian fell. His companions helped him to his feet and for a time, with their assistance, he kept upright. But there was a limit to their own strength and when they could no longer support him his legs couldn't bear his weight and he fell to the ground, unable to move.

An angry guard prodded him repeatedly but he was totally exhausted. While one guard unlocked the chain, two others picked him up. We turned to watch him being dragged, half-dead, towards the sledges where we thought he might continue the journey. But this didn't happen. When the guards returned, laughing and joking with each other, he was nowhere to be seen. Six people disappeared in this way during the second day. I was so curious about their fate that eventually I plucked up courage to ask one of the guards what had happened to the bodies.

'We need only their clothes as proof of their existence,' he answered. 'The wolves out there have got to be fed, otherwise they'll attack the convoy and you'll all die. That's why we try to reach the barracks before nightfall. If you look closely you'll see animal tracks. The wolves are never far away, following the convoy night and day, knowing they'll be fed. If I were you I wouldn't ask questions – it's a waste of energy and you'll end up like one of those corpses.'

By the fourth day we had travelled ninety miles, almost half the journey, but we had lost about thirty prisoners, each body having been stripped and left in the deep snow for the wolves to devour once we had disappeared from sight. We were now troubled by frostbite as well. Many prisoners were near death's door and there would have been many more deaths if we hadn't suddenly arrived at a small settlement situated on the banks of a frozen lake. To general amazement our chains were unlocked. The number of casualties had panicked the guards. Their orders were to ensure that the entire contingent arrived safe and well and ready to start work immediately. Already, however, thirty lives had been lost and the remaining 270 men were quite unfit for work.

Our diet was changed again to the more welcoming gruel and hot water and there were quite good rations compared with the barrack stops. After our meal we just flopped onto the floor for a well-earned sleep. I noticed that my arms and legs were swollen and lifeless so I rubbed them to try to get the circulation moving. Curling up into a ball I wrapped my coat around my feet, trying to create a cocoon of warmth. Sleep was shallow since the cold penetrated my whole body and chilled my soul. Perhaps that was a blessing; I felt that if I'd slept deeply I might never have woken up.

Suddenly the Mongolians, ever impatient, were waking us up with kicks and blows so that we could form an audience for an official-looking Russian visitor. He was wearing a number of medals on his thick fur overcoat. My brain could not make sense of his views. He seemed to be lecturing us on the magnificent progress of Soviet Communism and the virtues of Stalin as the father of the Soviet workers. We, he insisted, were among the privileged few who were being allowed to help him carry out his task of establishing better communications throughout his beloved country. Pacing up and down in front of us, his hands clasped behind his back, he glared at us with contempt. Suddenly, unable to stand the humiliation any longer, a Russian prisoner pushed his way to the front.

'If Stalin is so wonderful let him come here and see for himself his fantastic achievements. Here are 300 of his so-called children, hungry, lousy and numb with cold, our arms and legs swollen, some of us close to death. Yet we're forced to trek across these frozen wastes, sleeping on cement floors in makeshift barrack rooms, existing on gruel. How can we be Stalin's beloved children? So far my friend, we've lost thirty lives. Has Stalin grieved this loss? Does he know that thirty of his children have been left in the forest, stripped of their clothing, as fodder for the wolves? Of course he doesn't. Loss of life means nothing to you people. As far as you're concerned, we're just animals, work horses, serving the progress of Communism.'

Four guards entered the room. There was a terrific struggle and the prisoner was manhandled out of the door, still condemning the Russian proletariat and Stalin's rule. Dragged away, he was never seen again but he inspired his fellow prisoners who, with some effort, clapped and praised his courage. To them he was a hero who would die for his heroism.

Outside, the snow had begun to fall heavily, continuing throughout the day until it was rumoured to be four feet deep. A conference was held between the Mongolian guards and the Russian officials. The latter thought it unwise to risk the lives of the horses since replacements were hard to come by so far north. The Mongolians, with their usual impatience, were anxious to be off. It was decided to rest the convoy for one more day but two days passed and still we did not start. We prayed for more snow, the deeper the better, since each day's delay was an extra day's rest.

However, on the third morning after a long consultation between the guards and officials, it was decided to start again.

This time it was decided that a sledge would lead each convoy and would be attached to the prisoners' chains by a rope to assist us through the snow. This method soon proved to be useless and it became obvious that the journey was too slow and that we should never have ventured out. Fifteen more prisoners died, their bodies stripped and left for the wolves who, sensing the smell of death, still followed our footsteps.

The convoy got smaller each day. To our difficulties in reaching the barracks before nightfall was added the extra danger of the wolves attacking us in the darkness. Eventually we reached the stage where we could not continue without complete rest. The guards themselves and the horses were equally exhausted. It was agreed that we should spend a whole day and night in the next sparse barrack rooms. In fact, without our knowing it, fate had stepped in to save us all from sudden death. Huge storm clouds were gathering in the east and by late afternoon the Siberian winds had uprooted trees and whipped the snow into a frenzy, piling it into a mountain against the barrack walls and onto the roof.

In the dark the sound of the wind was horrifying. Suddenly the building began to creak and move and without warning the pressure of the snow began to split the wood. Within seconds eight of our companions were buried in the snow. Our chains hampered any rescue attempts and the guards, panic-stricken, freed us from our bonds whilst other prisoners dug in the snow in an attempt to free their friends. The guards, thinking that we would all perish, tried to dig an escape route through the avalanche. In the confusion two prisoners grabbed the guards' rifles and fired into the semi-darkness, killing one guard and injuring another. The remaining guards opened fire, killing in their turn the two armed prisoners and an innocent bystander.

When order was finally restored, the injured guard was shot by his colleagues since he was unable to push his body through the manmade tunnel and in any case they had no room for him on a sledge. Evidently these sadistic people would not tolerate injury even among their fellow guards. We were ordered to leave our buried friends and walk in orderly fashion out of the collapsed building. We were squeezed into the second barrack room, having to lean on one another as there was no room to sit down.

The following day we were re-chained and ordered out into the freezing cold. The winds had died down but the snow had blown into huge mountain-like drifts. We followed the sledges like robots, each of us fighting to stay alive. Many more lost the battle and collapsed, and were left for dead. The sledge was weighed down with the clothing of the victims. That was proof that we had indeed set out from Moscow with 300 men.

# Chapter Eleven

## *Pechora Camp*

Pechora Camp, when we finally reached it, was a disappointment to me. I had, without any rational justification, imagined a village within prison walls, spacious but escape-proof. The true picture was rather different. Instead of a village there was a network of newly-built barrack blocks, with wooden observation and guard towers rising into the sky. The whole area was surrounded by a double bank of barbed wire. And for miles and miles around there was nothing but forest and snow. This was my new home but, as I was soon to discover, not exactly an oasis in the desert.

The convoy came to a halt as each section waited to be taken through the only entrance, the guards clutching the papers that had travelled with us from Moscow. Names were checked off the list and the numbers added up. They confirmed that 85 of our group had perished on the long trek from the railhead. The surviving 215 of the commissar's quota were totally exhausted, more ready for the grave than for arduous work. Our hands were covered in frostbite, our legs swollen and our stomachs empty. Unsightly and stinking, we didn't give a damn. Hardly a promising labour cadre to help Stalin fulfil his five-year plan!

Huddled together in one room, we waited for the commissar. He arrived in all his splendour surrounded by personal guards. An order to stand to attention rang out through the room. We ignored it, since we were physically incapable of obeying. The commissar's name was Kurylo. Small in stature, only about five feet two inches tall, he compensated for this by the power of his voice. Turning on the Mongolian lieutenant, he shouted:

'Where are my workers? I wanted 300 men to start work today. What have I got? Two hundred and fifteen, and they're half dead and fit for nothing. Where are the rest? I need more and I want an explanation and a full report. I shall have to ask Moscow for more prisoners immediately. I can't fulfil my work plan with this trash!'

His voice rose higher and higher. Terrified, the lieutenant explained that the weather had been so severe that many had died en route and then, after the storms, there'd been a rebellion and two of his soldiers had been shot in a fierce battle with the prisoners. At this, one brave prisoner laughed out loud and daringly explained what had really happened at the time of the shootings. Kurylo gave him a long stare and took him to one side, speaking quietly to him. Quickly establishing the facts, he called the guards and the prisoner was led away. Kurylo then turned back to us with a warning that people who spoke their minds were dangerous and did not last long in his camp. I decided there and then that my mouth would remain shut. I would watch everything and say nothing. In those first few hours I realised that, to survive, I would have to keep a clear head and look for a chance to escape from this hell-hole.

Kurylo and his entourage left as abruptly as they'd arrived and we were left to await events. Once again we were de-loused and cleaned up. Fresh clothes were issued and we were each given a portion of bread and gruel followed by hot water. When we'd finished Kurylo returned with his personal guards, but this time accompanied by the Lescompros commissar who stood on a small rostrum to address us.

'We are the pioneers,' he began. 'These barracks will eventually hold fifteen hundred men but our work's behind schedule. The work is varied; we need men in the forests and the brick factory but above all we need carpenters to build the barracks. Each person will have a daily ration of food. The rules are quite simple here: the more work you do, the more food you get. Maybe you've seen a large area on the perimeter of the camp. This is the burial

71

ground and there are roughly 800 bodies buried there. These were people who wouldn't co-operate or who couldn't cope with the terrible winters here. Now you have the facts, it's up to you to turn them to your advantage.'

He stepped down from the rostrum and Kurylo took his place to announce that he'd managed to persuade the authorities to give us three days of rest and recuperation. But after that there must be non-stop work. Meanwhile we'd be divided up into various work parties which would start work immediately the three days were up. Volunteers were sought for the brick-works and building the barracks. I said nothing and was therefore consigned to forest work.

The rest period passed all too quickly and at 6 a.m. on the fourth morning, we new forestry workers were directed into the large room where the Lescompros commissar was waiting impatiently to deliver his final sermon.

'This is a food ticket,' he said, waving a piece of paper in the air. 'Without it you can't eat. You'll get it only after your work has been checked. The normal workload per person is approximately six cubic metres of timber per day. Each tree has to be felled, trimmed and cut into the right lengths. If you reach or exceed the norm you'll be entitled to the full food ration – one loaf of bread, soup and vegetables, hot water and one cube of sugar. But if you produce less than the norm you'll get only one piece of bread, clear soup and hot water. If your performance doesn't improve, you'll get less and less food until you end up in the cemetery. If you break the laws here you'll be punished by death. Don't forget, without a meal ticket you're as good as dead. And starvation's a nasty way to die.

'You'll be given your tools every morning when you leave the compound and you'll be responsible for them until you return in the evening when they'll be taken from you and counted. You'll be allocated your own work area and it's up to you to finish your work in this area as soon as you can if we are going to meet our targets for our great leader, Stalin.

'These are the facts you need to know. Now go to work. The guards will escort you to the forest. Remember what I've said, no work, no food. Quite simple.'

My mind was quite alert as I trudged the well-worn path into the forest but my body was still weak. Three days was too short a time to restore my strength. Just carrying the axe and the bowsaw was an effort and the thought of felling trees filled me with alarm. It was just as I expected and feared. My arms soon began to ache and my body, wet with sweat, cried out for mercy as I put every ounce of strength into the work. Once the tree was down, I stripped off its branches, putting them on one side to be burned. Felling and cleaning three trees and cutting the wood into lengths took me well into the afternoon and I had no chance of reaching my norm. I called a nearby guard who hurriedly checked my work and beckoned to the inspector. He in turn immediately stamped my logs as 'passed' and marked my meal ticket accordingly. I picked up my branches and started to burn them, the heat from the fire drying my perspiration and warming my blood. All the while I kept a close eye on the guards and inspectors.

It soon became apparent that only the inspectors were allowed to stamp the ends of the logs and the meal tickets. The guards did the measuring and often some time elapsed between the measuring and the stamping. Moreover, the guards seemed slow-witted and the inspectors were under constant pressure as they hurried from prisoner to prisoner stamping their work. I decided to try out a theory. While the guards were preoccupied, I sawed one centimetre off the stamped ends of a few of my logs and threw them on the fire. When I was sure they'd burned I carried on working. The following day, when work resumed, I already had these few logs to add to my norm. Having succeeded in cheating once I realised that I could, with care, cheat on a regular basis, thus reaching my norm without too much effort. I desperately needed time to regain my strength but I also needed as much food as possible to nourish my wasted body.

We worked throughout the bitterly cold winter months,

trudging back to the camp late at night, eating, sleeping and beginning the whole process again at six o'clock the following morning. Conversation was minimal as each prisoner tried to conserve his energy. The casualty rate was already high and the cemetery grew fuller by the day.

When conversation did take place it was only to discuss one of the many horror stories circulating in the camp. We heard that boardcutters had the highest death rate. They'd been chosen from men who had admitted to being joiners and carpenters. Their task was to convert our logs into planks, which had to be of exact dimensions since they were used in the building of barracks. The norm for this type of work was twenty planks a day but it was extremely rare for anyone to achieve it. Pig-headedly, the authorities refused to reduce the number, preferring to let the prisoners die. Gradually, through lack of food, the boardcutters became weaker until they were unable to lift the eight-foot saw, which weighed between fifteen and twenty pounds. At this stage there was no hope for them. Eventually they collapsed from starvation and made their final journey to the graveyard.

The grave-diggers also had a high death rate. Their norm was eight graves a day irrespective of the number of bodies for burial.

The Russians believed in being prepared, preferring to have enough empty graves to meet an increase in demand. The diggers had the additional demoralising task of burying the dead. Many times on our daily trek back to the barracks, we could see them dragging the naked corpses from the mortuary before throwing them in the graves and covering them with frozen soil.

Suddenly, summer arrived and the snow began to melt. The swollen Pechora river overflowed its banks and flooded parts of the forest. This was the time to send many of our logs downstream to other camps being built even deeper in the forests. My regular inspector was anxious. He and I had become quite friendly during the past months. He had regularly warmed himself by my fire and I had helped him in his calculations, to my advantage, many times. Now, having done his final check, he found he had a discrepancy of several thousand metres. Obviously I was not the only one who had been cheating. He was, understandably, distressed since his superiors could bring a charge of sabotage against him when they checked the figures. The prospect of ending up on the other side of the fence felling trees depressed him deeply.

Assuring him that his calculations were correct, I suggested that he tell his superiors straightaway that owing to the rapid increase in the flow of the river, many logs had been swept away by the flood. Relieved by my suggestion, he immediately informed the camp authorities, who accepted this explanation. As a result I was free to continue my cheating.

Despite my regular food allowance, I was still hungry but now that the snow had melted I could experiment with the various natural foods available in the forest. I first tried the sap of the fir trees but it contained too much resin and upset my stomach, causing vomiting, and making me hungrier than ever. I decided instead to sample beech sap. This experiment proved successful in keeping the pangs of hunger at bay. Also, since beech sap is intoxicating, I spent most of the summer in a rather high state.

At this time an infestation of lice was sweeping through the camp. Cholera and typhoid were closely linked with the infestation, and the camp authorities were worried for their own health. At an emergency meeting of commissars, it was decided that de-lousing operations would have to be stepped up. Two prisoners, one a medical student from Kiev University, were appointed as de-lousing agents. Their task was to fetch water from the Pechora river and wash and disinfect thoroughly the clothing of dead prisoners. They were also responsible for heating the water up in huge cauldrons, transferring it to the kegs and de-lousing the prisoners. Even they were set norms, fifty prisoners to be deloused per day. Every morning the names of prisoners who were required to stay in the barracks were called out in alphabetical order. Eventually my name was called and I was sent in a batch of ten to the special de-lousing room. We took off our clothes and threw them into pungent-smelling liquid. Then we had to step into a keg of foul-smelling water. We were told to submerge our whole body, keeping our eyes tightly closed since the chemicals could damage our sight. After being fully submerged, we were helped out and put in a keg of clear warm water. Clean clothing was then issued and we were taken back to the barracks. We treated the day as a holiday since it was the only day we ever had off. When the end of the alphabet was reached the whole process began again.

Unfortunately the one de-lousing day per month did not solve the problem since we slept in the same room as men who had not yet been deloused. Lice move quickly, especially onto clean heads. They grew immune to the chemicals and within a couple of days we were all infested again. We had a hot stove in our room and after our evening meal we'd sometimes take off our shirts and wrap them round the hot pipes listening to the pop, pop, pop as the lice died from the heat. Another sport was to see how many we could kill between our nails. One evening I counted 72 before getting bored with the game. Lice, hunger, cold and heavy work were the constant features of our lives. But there was an even greater danger, the Camp Commandant.

He seemed to have unrestricted authority. He could shoot any prisoners on sight, for any reason. He held each prisoner's life in his hands. Our first encounter with this sadist occurred on Easter Sunday. Since this day is one of the main Russian holidays we had asked for a day off work, but without success. The prisoners became agitated. Word spread that there would be a rebellion on Easter Day, and that the prisoners would refuse to work even if this meant foregoing their meal allowance.

At six o'clock on Easter Day morning the order to get up echoed through the barracks. This morning it was totally ignored and no one stirred from his bunk. Some of the prisoners started singing Easter hymns and others joined in so that quite soon all the prisoners, 1,000 of them, were part of the choir. The guards, unable to restore any semblance of order, disappeared to report the disturbance to Kurylo. Furious because this action was disturbing his rest day, he ordered the guards to assemble the prisoners in the camp square so that he could address them. Any prisoners disobeying this order would be shot.

Twenty minutes later, in full battledress, bayonets attached to their rifles, the guards returned to the singing prisoners. One shot was fired and there was instant silence. The orders were given and we had no alternative but to obey. Reluctantly we left our beds, dressed and were escorted into the square. I noticed that in the observation towers the guards were manning machine-guns, with the sights trained on the prisoners. A makeshift platform had been hurriedly erected and a table had been placed by the entrance to the army quarters.

Kurylo appeared, his face like thunder, four Mongolian soldiers surrounding him. He stood on the platform with two guards on either side, their guns trained on the crowd, their fingers itching to pull the trigger. He began to speak, the usual political speech which by now we all knew off by heart. He was very conscious of his small stature and as his voice grew louder he leapt on to the table. His voice went down an octave.

'You owe me your lives, each and every one of you. Who feeds you? Who gives you warm clothing, you lazy bastards? Is this the way you repay my hospitality, putting your work beneath some stupid religious belief? Who is more important, your stupid God or me?' His voice began to rise again.

'I know who's responsible for this disturbance and they'll be punished.'

He scanned the crowd.

'You.'

He pointed to one of the tallest men.

'You. You. You.'

He picked out six of the tallest men and lined them up in front of him.

'In the name of Stalin, shoot the bastards.'

The guards raised their guns and we could only look on in horror.

'Wait, first bring them spades, let them dig their own graves.'

Two guards hurriedly disappeared into the building, returning with six spades. We stood rooted to the spot, not believing what was happening in front of our eyes.

'Dig, dig,' urged the guards. Having witnessed Kurylo's wrath on many occasions they knew he was not bluffing. Meanwhile Kurylo had calmed down. From his pocket he took a packet of *machorka*, a strong Russian tobacco and a piece of newspaper and proceeded to roll a cigarette.

'When I've finished this cigarette, your graves should be deep enough. I'll take great pleasure in watching you die.'

He took a long drag on his cigarette, blowing the smoke towards the horror-stricken prisoners. The hole was roughly two feet deep as he slowly inhaled for the last time. Stubbing the cigarette end on the table, he asked:

'Who's got the most power now, you, me or your God? Somehow I don't see Him intervening to save you.'

He pointed at the guards.

'Shoot them!'

The guards opened fire and all six prisoners were mown down in front of our eyes, innocent victims of the Soviet regime. Six lives taken in vain on that Easter Sunday.

Kurylo was shouting again.

'Come forward all those who prefer to pray instead of working! Come forward now!'

There were no volunteers. Silently we formed into our work parties. As I passed the bodies, I secretly made the sign of the cross and whispered a silent prayer.

An air of despondency hung over the forest, even the inspectors were silent. I attacked each tree as if it were Kurylo, sinking the saw into the trunk, imagining it was Kurylo's neck, the sap his life-blood trickling down the stump. It was the safest way to rid myself of my pent-up emotions as I relived the events of the morning over and over again.

By now the short summer was well underway and owing to the

swollen river the transportation of logs was considerably behind schedule. To save time it was decided that forestry workers should camp out on the river bank to ensure an early start each morning. In this work accidents were frequent. One slip off the moving ramps and you were lost in the swirl of the waters. In fact many took the chance to drown themselves in this way. I often thought I'd do the same if life became unbearable. I noticed that the guards seemed unperturbed by these deaths, perhaps because less space would be taken up in the cemetery.

Our rations were often late in arriving and I was perpetually hungry. One day, as I helped stack logs on the river bank, I noticed a barge moored to a makeshift wooden jetty. It was a supply barge and the Mongolian guards were busy helping to unload it. There was an overpowering smell of fish. Unaware that he was being watched, one of the guards picked up a fish and banged it against the boat until its head fell off. He then began to eat it, looking up as he did so. Seeing me watching him, he smiled, showing his yellow teeth and holding out the half-eaten fish. I told him I couldn't eat raw fish.

'You'll eat anything if you're hungry. Here, take it!'

It was a friendly gesture. Fearing reprisals if I threw kindness in his face I took a bite. I obviously did the right thing because he quickly handed me two more raw fish, which I hid. After our meal that night, when the fire was lit to dry off our wet clothes, we fried the fish and ate heartily, relishing our first taste of fried fish in years.

## Chapter Twelve

# *Escapes and Punishments*

Every prisoner's dream was to break free from the misery and degradation of the penal camps. But the chances of escape were remote. Hundreds of miles of forests, hungry packs of wolves, the bitter cold, knee-deep snow and army patrols stood between a would-be escaper and freedom. Even if a town or a railway were reached, a prisoner on the run could expect no help from ordinary Russians, who often preferred to turn informer if they could obtain some improvement in their own lives. In these desperate times people were even ready to testify against their own families if it meant an extra loaf of bread or some otherwise unobtainable delicacy.

My dream was no different. I hated Siberia and slavery. I had been born free in the mountains of Poland. The only reason I survived in these wild, desolate forests was my iron will and my determination to become a free man again.

Yet there were very few examples of successful escapes. The punishments for failure were horrific, much more terrifying than the usual bullet through the neck. Each prisoner had his own pitiable story to tell. For example, in our barracks was a young Russian named Vaska. He was a very impulsive, hot-headed youth who came from Astrakhan, in the Kalmukistan province, on the Caspian Sea. He had been well-liked and capable and could turn his hand to anything. The local NKVD officer had been very impressed with him and had offered him a supervisory job on a collective farm on condition that he reported any suspicious conversations to the authorities.

Worse still, he was told that he was expected to monitor the conversations of his girlfriend, Katiusha, who was employed on the farm. When he refused, the NKVD dragged him from his bed late one night and arrested him. Charged with counter-revolutionary activities he eventually joined us at Pechora Camp. He was absolutely determined to escape. During that first spring when the river was at its height and we were camping in the forest to increase our output he decided it was now or never. On the evening of the fish supper he decided to slip away.

In the darkness he jumped into the swollen river and managed to swim to the opposite bank. He hoped that the guards would presume him dead since the death rate from drowning was high at that time of year. For days he tried to find a path away from the riverside but the river had overflowed and the area was a mass of bogs and swamps. He was not fit enough to survive without food and knew nothing about the natural foods to be found in the forest. Wet, hungry, exhausted and quite desperate he collapsed on the riverbank only to be found by the river patrols. Dragged back to the camp he was given an audience with Commissar Kurylo.

Kurylo paced round him, his voice rising higher and higher as he lectured him on the evils of attempting to escape. Told that the punishment must fit the crime, Vaska was ordered into the square and told to start digging. For two whole days he dug until the hole was two metres deep. The guard, closely followed by Kurylo, arrived to inspect the hole. Vaska tottered on the edge waiting for the bullet in the neck to put him out of his misery. Kurylo smiled sadistically and motioned to the guards. Suddenly one guard lunged forward, knocking Vaska into the pit. Quickly a heavy wooden cover was dragged across the opening, sealing off any hope of escape.

He spent a week in this isolation. His only food was a slice of bread pushed through a small gap once a day. Death crept up on him slowly. Wanting to die and having nothing to lose he started shouting at the guards, calling them 'Mongolian bastards' and other obscene names. They totally ignored him until the following day. This time, instead of the usual slice of bread, two live rats were dropped into the hole 'to keep you company' as the guard said.

Two more weeks passed and still Vaska was alive. Kurylo was astounded and decided to see for himself. The cover was removed. Looking down on that wasted, partly naked body, even Kurylo took pity on him and ordered the guards to bring him out. They put some clothes on his trembling body and gave him bread and water, but he could not swallow. His arms and legs were stiff with cold. That night he was returned to our barracks.

The following day, with the loving word Katiusha on his lips, Vaska died. His only consolation was that he had spent his last night in the arms of his friends. Learning of his death, Kurylo ordered him to be buried in the hole he had dug, along with three other prisoners who had also died during that night. I often think about that innocent and brave youth, whose love of freedom cost him his life.

New consignments of prisoners arrived each month replacing the manpower lost through suicide, sickness, starvation and execution by the guards. Among the most recent contingent of prisoners were four Uzbekhs. It was obvious that they were very close friends, helping one another and sharing their food if one of them hadn't reached the work norm. They worked alongside me, manoeuvring a huge double saw, felling trees more than one metre in diameter. Owing to their quick tempers, they were forever falling foul of the guards. At this time the winter months were just beginning and the snow was deepening daily. As a result our work was hindered and progress was slow.

The Uzbekhs called the guards over to measure their work. There followed a heated dispute about how many logs one of the men had cut. The guard turned on the offender. One of his friends, sure that his companion was about to be shot, picked up an axe and leapt towards the guard. As the guard turned, the axe struck his neck so forcefully that it completely severed his head from his body. Everything happened so quickly. The Uzbekhs grabbed the gun and ammunition and disappeared into the forest. The inspector alerted the other guards who set off in pursuit but the snow was falling so fast that it obliterated the tracks of the fugitives. The search was abandoned although a general alert was relayed to all the army units scattered along the Pechora river.

Not hearing anything about the men for a whole week, we assumed they'd escaped. We were about to celebrate their success when word reached us that they'd been caught, but only after a good fight. After exposure to the elements for almost a week they'd been surprised while resting in a makeshift shelter. Though surrounded, they had opened fire, killing two more soldiers and injuring three others.

Normally the soldiers shot all escaping prisoners but this time Commissar Kurylo had given special orders that the fugitives were to be returned to Pechora Camp as soon as possible. Apparently he'd decided to make a public spectacle of their punishment to act as a deterrent to the other prisoners. This meant ignoring all the rules. Kurylo did not consult the NKVD or the other commissars. He seemed confident that the mere mention that he'd attended school with Stalin himself was authorisation enough to proceed. The punishment he devised was the product of his sadistic mind and his vivid imagination.

On their return to the camp, the escapees were thrown naked into the isolators, a series of single cages big enough for one person, to await their execution. Sunday was then declared a public holiday so that prisoners and guards could witness the reprisals for the murder of three of Stalin's 'loyal soldiers', as they were called. In the centre of the square an eight-foot pole was erected and a cartwheel fastened to the top. From the wheel hung four strong ropes each ending in a noose. Barbed wire was spread across the ground around the pole and was then covered by white sheets.

At seven o'clock on Sunday morning, we were herded into the square. Kurylo arrived at eight, splendidly dressed in plush red trousers, white shirt and red tie. He ordered his table to be moved to within inches of the barbed wire. Turning to face his audience, he launched into one of his usual sermons, praising Soviet Communism and the high standard of living enjoyed by the Soviet people. He congratulated himself on his untiring efforts to make the working conditions in Pechora Camp so agreeable.

'Show me one other camp where bread can be obtained so easily. No prisoner who works hard is denied what he needs to live.'

His voice began to rise with excitement as he turned to the condemned prisoners, still encaged in their isolators.

'I've treated them as my own sons and what thanks do I get? Three of my best guards killed in cold blood. So, I'll take a death for a death as a warning to all of you here that rebellion won't be tolerated. Bring the bastards here.'

The naked prisoners were manhandled into the square by six Mongolian soldiers, four carrying rifles, one carrying a hammer and the other a sickle. At the execution post, nooses were placed round their necks and tightened.

Kurylo stood on his table.

'These four bastards desecrated the red flag by killing three of Stalin's honoured guards. I've ordered it to be re-painted with their blood. For the glory of our beloved Stalin let the execution begin!'

At this the two guards carrying the hammer and the sickle started to swing their weapons at the naked prisoners, forcing them to run in a circle across the white sheet covering the barbed wire. Their feet were cut to shreds as the hammer rained blows on their bodies and the sickle cut deep wounds in their flesh. I felt revulsion and disgust and turned away. How long could they endure this torture and humiliation?

One prisoner stumbled and fell. Like a vulture, the Mongolian wielding the sickle pounced on the body, looking towards Kurylo for the signal to kill. We turned towards Kurylo, our eyes begging him for mercy but, flushed with pleasure and excitement, he turned his thumb downwards. Immediately the sickle separated the prisoner's head from his convulsing body. With hysterical laughter the guard began to paint the four corners of the sheet with the dripping blood. When his lust had been satisfied, he kicked the head in the direction of the guard wielding the hammer, who proceeded to smash the skull into an unrecognisable pulp.

These horrific scenes were repeated as each prisoner received the same treatment. Kurylo continued to watch with an evil smile spreading across his face.

As soon as this nauseating spectacle was over, we were ordered back to work, each of us reflecting on our fate if we were caught attempting to escape. Some good at least came out of the incident. One month after these horrible executions, NKVD headquarters in Moscow was informed about the incident. Kurylo was ordered to Moscow and, after a long inquiry and interrogation, he was shot, along with his two Mongolian henchmen. Yet in the following years, whenever I saw the red Soviet flag, I saw also the hammer of the NKVD, the sickle of the Politburo and the red blood of innocent people fighting for their freedom. And I thought about the millions who lost their lives in the Siberian camps. Their blood will stain that flag forever.

After witnessing this horrific event, I was in no doubt that any escape, to be successful, would have to be planned carefully and well in advance. Also, though I should have to take every pre-caution to avoid capture, in the event of failure I had to have the means available to take my own life if necessary.

By this time I had been at Pechora Camp for nearly two years and knew that I wouldn't last another winter. Security had recently been stepped up and there was a clamp-down on the inspectors since too many people were found to have been cheating the system. If I could not escape, my only other option was to take my own life. However, my religious upbringing led me to reject this course as contrary to God's will.

In order to clarify my thoughts, I took up my old habit of meditating during the evenings. As a result, I decided to place my fate entirely in God's hands. I concluded that it was worth risking my life in order to gain my freedom.

# Chapter Thirteen

# *A New Career*

It was late autumn 1941. Each time a new consignment of prisoners arrived we were anxious to obtain news of the outside world. We were staggered to hear of the war between Hitler and Stalin which was then in full swing. We learned that on 22 June 1941 Germany had attacked the Soviet Union with 190 divisions and numerous tanks and aircraft. Together with Italian and Finnish troops, the German shock formations of tanks and motorised convoys penetrated the outer flanks of the Soviet army. The Red Army had no choice but to beat a hasty retreat as Hitler's forces pressed on towards Moscow.

The news of the invasion was greeted with delight in the camp. Even the Russian prisoners celebrated since they all felt betrayed by the Communist regime. A German victory, they believed, would bring freedom from the hated commissars and the poisonous lies of Soviet propaganda.

I too was filled with new hope by the German invasion. I could speak German fluently, far better than most Russians. I was convinced that the Germans would win. I knew the cruelties of Hitler's Gestapo from the early days of the war in Poland, but what I had seen in the labour camps and prisons of the Soviet Union was far more outrageous. I preferred to take my chances against the Germans than face a slow death by starvation in the forests of Siberia.

A general mobilisation was already underway throughout the Soviet Union. Orders were sent to every camp demanding that all young able-bodied guards, officers, technicians and maintenance men be drafted to the front. Older men replaced them. Food rations were drastically reduced; supplies became irregular and arguments arose among the prisoners. Some turned informer to get more food. Prisoners who still managed to cheat at work or who openly discussed their escape plans were denounced to the authorities. Fighting among the prisoners broke out regularly. The situation was becoming desperate and I soon learned it was foolish to confide in my companions.

The army was naturally given priority in the distribution of food but this exacerbated the existing shortages in the camps. Many an evening, after a hard day's work in the forest, we were given only hot water and a slice of bread, the only food available. A shortage of hay led to the starvation of many of the horses but their deaths were welcomed since their carcasses could be utilised by the cooks. Stews and soups were on the menu for a whole week after the death of a horse. In desperation the guards shot and killed some of the wolves which roamed around the perimeter of the camp. Eventually they too disappeared, knowing their fate if they came within shooting range. Work fell behind schedule once prisoners refused to work hard, knowing there would be no increase in rations for those who achieved targets. Many were shot for their insubordination.

I survived these harrowing months by losing myself in my dreams, dreams that the Germans would penetrate the forests and free us, dreams where I was running out of the forests into the arms of civilisation. Through my dreams I began to formulate a plan of escape. I continued to meditate at night to keep my mind alert.

The lack of food and the general disobedience caused the commissar serious problems and he eventually called a meeting with the General Commandant in charge of all the forestry camps. The following morning we were all ordered into the yard before work to hear a lecture from the Commandant on disobedience. But threatening hungry, dying prisoners with the death penalty was a waste of time. Death was a blessing that any one of us at that time would have welcomed. Looking at the gaunt, emaciated prisoners, he must have known we were all fighting a losing battle. But then came another announcement of far more significance to me.

He asked how many prisoners were serving a ten-year sentence. I raised my hand with the others. How many of us had a basic knowledge of the maintenance of telephone lines, was the next question. Apparently most telephone technicians had been called to Moscow to help in the city's defence. This time I kept my hand down.

'Anyone with such knowledge will be guaranteed a better, much easier job,' he went on. 'My orders stipulate that only prisoners serving a ten-year sentence can volunteer. Have we any such people in this camp? It's a chance for you to better yourselves.'

No hands were raised. Of course I knew about the maintenance of telephone lines from my time in Signals in the Polish Army. But I was not sure what to do. My mind was racing. Was this the chance I'd been waiting for? Should I raise my hand, take a chance? Would I get more freedom, perhaps even enough to plan an escape? I raised my hand. Looking round, I noticed about ten other hands raised in the air. Six of us were asked to stay behind when the rest of the prisoners were sent back to work.

I paced up and down. Had I done the right thing? Had I bitten off more than I could chew? I tried to convince myself that it was better to take the job since I couldn't be less free than I was already. I hated the thought of dying as a lumberman in the wastes of Siberia. For the first time in years, I knew the feeling of excitement as I waited for an interview with the Commandant, the Soviet 'giver and taker of life'. He saw us one by one. Sitting behind his huge table, he motioned me to sit down and offered me a cigarette, a luxury I had not tasted in two years. The smoke filling my lungs made me feel quite heady, owing to my lack of food. He asked me my name, nationality and the nature of my crime.

I told him the truth and he listened to me for an hour, offering me another cigarette, a drink of vodka and a piece of chocolate.

The drawer by his side from which these delicacies were extracted was like a magician's box. I felt, in that hour, that I had practically convinced him of my innocence. He sympathised with me and promised me help.

However, authorisation for my removal from the camp had to be approved by the NKVD. Since prisoners working on the telephone lines enjoyed considerable freedom, only those who could be trusted were employed. Had I been Russian there would have been no problem, but my Polish nationality caused complications. They eventually told me I'd have to have another interview, this time with an NKVD officer.

Three days later, while at work in the forest, I was ordered to return to camp for my interview. Behind the table in the Commissar's room sat an NKVD captain, looking quite resplendent in his uniform, his polished medals glistening in the light of the lamp.

In front of him on the table lay his revolver, the symbol of his authority. Next to the revolver, spread across the table, were my prison papers and signed confession. His approach was identical to that of the NKVD interrogator in the Lubianka. Again the offer of a cigarette and, while I inhaled the strong smoke, he thumbed through my papers.

'I will ask the questions,' he said. 'You will answer only when I ask you to speak. Do you understand?'

I nodded.

'What nationality are you, German or Polish? It's not very clear. You seem to have dual nationality. You may answer.'

I explained that I'd been born and raised in Poland and therefore I was Polish.

'Why, if you are Polish, do you speak Russian so fluently? I am Russian, I do not speak your language fluently. Please explain.'

I told him that Russian had been a recommended language at school and that I'd studied languages at college. I was fluent in several tongues.

'Now why do you want to work in communications? Why do

you know so much about telephone maintenance? Were you an officer in the Polish army? Answer.'

I said I'd been too young to be an officer but, having worked in Signals, I'd taken a course in telephone maintenance and knew something about telephone systems.

He nodded, offered me yet another cigarette and leaned back in his comfortable chair to study my answers. After several minutes he resumed his questioning.

'Think before you answer this question. These documents in front of me accuse you of spying yet you plead your innocence. Why sign your life away if, as you insist, you are innocent?'

I did not wish to offend anyone, least of all my inquisitor. I slowly began to explain.

'During my interrogation in the Lubianka I was depressed. It was my first time in prison and I was confused and bewildered. I was also young and desperate to get out. I signed the statement willingly, not realising the terrible mistake I was making.'

As I was speaking he rested his elbows on the table, cupping his chin in his hand. Thanking me when I'd finished, he suddenly stood up and withdrew into the main office, leaving me to finish my cigarette and to wonder what fate had in store for me. Half an hour later he returned, his expression as inscrutable as ever. Almost apologetically he said he couldn't get me released and I had to serve my ten years. But he could make my life easier by recommending me for a three-month trial as a telephone line repairer. If I could prove I could do the work, I'd be permitted to continue. But there was another condition – I had to agree to report on any anti-Communist activities, any suspect conversations, anything I heard which might damage the Soviet cause.

I found this proposal shocking, since informing was deeply repugnant to me. My first instinct was to jump to my feet, strike the desk and shout 'No!' But I stopped myself, remembering in time that this job was simply a cover until I could plan my escape. I could agree to anything because in the end I could please myself. Within three months I felt sure I'd be free. I asked about special privileges, extra food, a comfortable bed, a horse for my travels.

'All these conditions are included in this document. Don't worry. Help me and I'll help you. You understand?'

I nodded. He pushed the document across the table.

'Sign please.'

I picked up the document and started to read it. The captain became agitated and began to speak quickly.

'You do agree with my conditions, don't you? You're agreeing to report any counter-revolutionary activities that come to your notice. You'll also see that we've changed your name to Vasil. You must make all your reports in writing and sign them with this name. Is everything clear?'

I nodded as he pushed the pen towards me. With a trembling hand I signed. I'd once signed my death warrant; maybe now I was signing the document that would lead me to freedom.

The captain smiled. Producing a bottle of vodka, he offered me a glass.

'To our working relationship.' He sipped his drink. 'You'll travel with me tomorrow to Troitsko Pechorsk, a large settlement in the north. This is where the NKVD headquarters for the area are located, as well as the Northern Forestry Central Office and the main telephone centre. But first you need some warm clothes, a good hot wash and some food.'

He escorted me to the washroom. The water was warm and inviting and I lingered while I washed away the misery of months of deprivation and hardship. I almost fell asleep in the bath but a sharp knock quickly brought me round. For one awful moment I felt as if I'd been caught red-handed doing something forbidden but it was only the guard waiting to take me to the stores to pick up my new clothes. To my amazement and pleasure, I was offered a pair of knee-high fleece-lined boots, new underwear, a thick working shirt, and a pair of thick padded trousers. To complete my wardrobe I was given a thick, padded, thigh-length jacket and a leather hat with padded flaps to protect my ears.

Having paraded up and down in my new gear, I was taken back to the captain's office. On the table was the largest amount of food I'd seen in years, white bread, sausage, ham, freshly cooked *pierogi* (similar to apple pie) and wine and vodka in abundance.

He invited me to join him and I ate like a man possessed. In the end he had to stop me in case I made myself ill. We finished the meal with a cup of hot strong tea. Afterwards he gave me a packet of Russian tobacco and a sheet of newspaper to act as cigarette paper. That night I slept in a proper bed. I felt like a prince.

The following day after a hearty breakfast I got ready for the journey and took my seat on the captain's sledge. As I sat waiting to leave I felt guilty at leaving behind all those desperate men in Pechora Camp. But at the same time I felt intense relief that the odds of my staying alive had lengthened. I reminded myself that in this desperate fight for survival it was every man for himself.

With a crack of the whip the journey began. As the huge gates opened to let us pass, I felt as if I was no longer a prisoner. I was exhilarated and happy but, in the furthest corner of my mind, tucked away for the present, was the fear of the unknown and the thought of having to spy on my fellow prisoners.

It was dusk when we arrived at Troitsko Pechorsk. I was handed over to the chief technician in charge of communications and the small telephone exchange. He took me to a dormitory where six beds lined the walls, each with a mattress and blankets. Catching me staring at the beds, the technician explained that, owing to the shortage of maintenance men there were only three men sharing the room at that time. Most of the younger men had been sent to the front and his oldest and most trusted friend had died only two weeks before when the bough of a tree broke under his weight when he was repairing a line. Having broken his leg in the fall, he was trying to crawl back to the camp when he was attacked by a pack of wolves. His body was later found by a search party.

I had many questions to ask but the journey had taken its toll and the sight of the beds made me long for sleep. I decided to keep my questions until the morning. As I pulled the blankets under my chin, thoughts of escape spun round and round in my head. I had to tell myself not to hurry. I had three months to plan a foolproof escape.

Intent on making an impression, I rose early and I prepared myself for my new job. My new acquaintance took me to one side. The working 'norm', he told me, was ten miles a day, and a horse would be provided. The telephone lines between the small Siberian settlements were primitive, usually strung from tree-top to tree-top and covered only with a thin coating of rubber for protection. The larger settlements had proper lines connected to poles erected alongside the forest paths. These were easier to keep fault-free and any fault could be traced more easily as you moved from pole to pole. Most of the faults were due to bad earthings, or breaks in the line as a result of heavy snowfalls or icing. As he finished explaining the basics of the job, I quickly realised that I had a sound knowledge of the work and that any difficult faults could be solved by a process of elimination.

When he'd given me the basic instruction, he issued me with a hand-operated telephone, a pole with a large hook on the end and a bag attached to a leather belt which contained all the basic tools, including the hooks needed for climbing the slippery poles. He gave me a last word of advice.

'Above all, don't hurry. Finding the fault is the most difficult part of the work, and the most important. It can sometimes take days. The repair itself is usually a minor matter and should only take a few minutes. The rule is, take your time and do a good job. You'll find it's not easy but at least your work'll be appreciated and you'll be treated fairly.'

With that he took me to see my horse; 'Sometimes the only friend you have to talk to during the whole day'. I followed him across the yard to the stables. Compared to the shattering labour I was used to in the forest, a repair man's job was a piece of cake. My prospects had improved out of recognition and I knew, deep down, that if I played my cards right I could escape.

# Chapter Fourteen

## *The Escape*

Siberia was in the grip of winter. Working outside in Arctic conditions, I travelled deep into the forests repairing broken telephone lines. My warm clothing, food and provisions, plus a small amount of money, were life-saving improvements over my existence in the camp at Pechora. But I couldn't forget that I was still a prisoner and prisoners were not issued with guns. So my only defence against the wolves and other wild animals was my axe.

My horse became my best friend, as I was told he would be. In retrospect I owed my life to him on more than one occasion. His instincts helped him to detect wild animals at a great distance and so he became for me a kind of early warning system. My many encounters, especially with wolves, led me to appeal to the NKVD captain for a rifle, but without success. He was bound by a strict NKVD rule that no prisoner, unless of Russian origin, could carry any type of firearm.

It took me at least a month to adjust to my new job since I had suffered so much, both mentally and physically, during my imprisonment in the camp. Now, with food and exercise, my physical condition began to improve but I wasn't yet ready to attempt an escape. I knew that if my escape were to be successful I would have to be in peak condition, not only physically but mentally as well. Before me was an enormous journey of 4,000 miles down towards the Afghan border. To prepare myself, I resumed my meditations. But this kind of mental preparation was insufficient. I needed a foolproof plan as well.

Fortunately I had a very good, even a photographic, memory. I spent some time studying parts of the huge map on the telephone exchange wall. In the privacy of my room I reproduced from memory a primitive map of the area, marking the various barracks, the rivers and tributaries, and the villages between Troitsko Pechorsk and the nearest railway station, Sosnogorsk, approximately 150 miles away.

I made notes of the length of time I was actually left on my own and tried to estimate how much time I would have before a search party was sent out to look for me. I prayed nightly, thanking God for my new job and for my escape from the hunger and degradation of Pechora Camp. I remembered in my prayers all my former comrades who would surely die there.

My repair work was constantly hampered by paths disappearing under huge snowdrifts and by fallen trees which had to be disposed of before I could continue my work. Whilst I was busy with my repairs, my horse would wait patiently for me, tethered to a nearby telegraph pole. I was constantly alerted to danger by his snorting and restlessness. If he pinned back his ears and looked agitated, I knew that danger was close at hand. The only thing to do was to ride away and return only when he felt it was safe.

One morning we were travelling to our first repair when my horse stopped. He then reared up and plunged off the path, racing headlong between the trees. Reining him to a standstill, I turned him back in the direction of the track where, to my horror, I saw a huge Siberian bear standing some fifty yards in front of me. Turning slowly, he ambled back into the forest, quite oblivious of the fright he had given us. My survival really depended on my horse and we became the best of friends, totally devoted to one other. For most of the time I had no one else to talk to so I talked to him, telling him of my plans to escape, stroking his nose and letting him nuzzle into my armpit.

Most of the settlements I visited were small hamlets whose peasant inhabitants treated me with kindness. The war had disrupted their lives. They would have liked to remain neutral but were forced to support the Soviet government since they depended on Troitsko Pechorsk for their food supplies. The villages were ideal places to pick up information to pass on to the NKVD but I was quite uninterested in this. My thoughts were dominated from dawn till dusk by the prospect of escape.

Once a week I had to make my report to the NKVD captain. Had I heard any whispers against the regime? What confidential telephone calls had I monitored whilst repairing the lines? Since I never had anything to report, he would press me harder each week, practically accusing me of non-cooperation. I tried to convince him that the people I came into contact with were ordinary peasants who didn't concern themselves with Communism or the war but were totally taken up by the daily struggle to keep their bodies warm and their stomachs full. My excuses weren't accepted.

'If you don't help me you'll be replaced, it's as simple as that,' he pointed out. 'There are plenty of volunteers ready to jump into your shoes, so if you don't want to return to Pechora Camp in disgrace, you've got to produce some results! Your three months will soon be up, so I'd think carefully about this if I were you.'

Apart from the interviews, life was bearable and I enjoyed my freedom. Having finished my quota for the day, I'd wander around the nearest town or village buying bread or tobacco, testing the reactions of the militia, imagining that I was actually on the run, sizing up situations. I learned a lot. Because I wore warm working clothes I was practically ignored by the militia and left very much to my own devices. After all, everyone knew that government jobs were only given to trusted informers.

When two months of my probation had passed, the time was ripe for my final preparations. I couldn't afford to make a mistake. On my home-made map I marked my proposed route, 150 miles through deep forests and across rivers and tributaries which, with a bit of luck, would be frozen at this time of the year. I'd be constantly in danger from wolves and bears. And this would only be stage one of my escape, to the railway station at Sosnogorsk.

Apart from wild animals I did not envisage any great problems on this part of the journey. A much greater challenge though would be getting into a southbound railway truck without being spotted. But I was pretty confident since I'd built up my strength through eating well, exercising and sleeping on comfortable beds. Furthermore I was mentally strong through my regime of regular meditations during the past two months. I was twenty-six years old and the adrenalin was flowing. All in all, I felt well-prepared for my forthcoming ordeal. I had many years to live and I'd no intention of wasting them in Siberia. From this moment I placed my life in the hands of God; only He knew my fate.

Newspapers were available in the larger settlements. They were always a few days old but the reports about the war were very useful to me. Millions of evacuees were moving east to take refuge in the Ural mountains region. The country seemed to be in chaos and I intended to take full advantage of it. Because I was 'trusted' I received a small amount of money each week to pay for provisions and accommodation; for example if I was unable to return to Troitsko Pechorsk and I had to sleep in one of the villages. Over the weeks I'd saved quite a lot of money, which I hoped would meet my needs until I reached the warmer south.

It was coming up to my weekly interview. I'd only two weeks left to provide some tangible evidence of espionage if I wanted to avoid being returned to the camp. I'd discussed my feelings with Ivan, my colleague, with whom I'd share a bottle of vodka from time to time. We used to have a chat between shifts. His job was to man the exchange during the night, noting any faults that might occur. At midnight he'd do a spot check to make sure all the lines were working, and the following morning I'd re-check before setting off with my list of repairs. Ivan warned me that the NKVD were already looking for a replacement for me since I'd not come up to expectations. I had to act fast. The thought of returning to the death camp spurred me on.

I began to put my escape plan into operation. I finished in the forest earlier than usual hoping that no one would be in the exchange. My luck was in. I hastily unscrewed the cover that protected the main apparatus and quickly cut through the lines that connected Troitsko Pechorsk to Sosnogorsk station, making sure they were severed as close to the terminal as possible to avoid detection. My heart was in my mouth as I struggled to replace the cover. The telephone exchange was centrally located and militia and NKVD men frequently dropped by to report telephone faults and to do spot checks on our work. When I'd finished, I knew that all I had to do was to stay cool and wait until morning.

Ivan arrived in jovial mood. He stamped the snow off his boots and blew warm air into his red hands.

'You look cold, Ivan,' I said. 'I know just the thing to warm you up.' Opening the cupboard, I brought out the vodka and two glasses. Drinking loosened Ivan up. He loved vodka but didn't know when to stop. I knew that if he drank too much, he'd forget the midnight check and my sabotage would go undetected. We drank until ten o'clock and I made sure that Ivan's glass was never empty. He began to feel drowsy and I knew he wouldn't stir until morning. Making him comfortable I returned to my room. Sleep came in fits and starts. Still fully clothed I tossed and turned, excited at the prospect of escape but anxious about the possibility of being recaptured.

When I returned to the exchange the following morning, Ivan was just beginning to wake up. Jovially I started re-checking the lines, calling each number separately, chatting to Ivan as I worked. I started to check the Sosnogorsk lines. Naturally they were dead.

'We have a fault, Ivan. Check in your book to see if these lines were working at midnight.'

Ivan checked his log book, realised that he'd not done his midnight check and hastily concealed this by writing in his report that all the lines had been working at midnight. Naturally he didn't want to get on the wrong side of the NKVD but his false report neatly covered my sabotage. Once this line failure was classed as a priority fault, I reported it without delay to the NKVD. They immediately authorised me to leave the settlement, giving me the official pass to stay overnight in the villages until the job was finished.

It was a clear crisp morning. I saddled my horse and stuffed provisions for two days into the saddle-bag. When I had worked on this line once before, it had taken me three days to locate the fault, repair it and return to the settlement. In the circumstances, two days of supplies seemed reasonable and wouldn't arouse suspicion. It seemed just like another working day as I waved goodbye to Ivan and headed towards the forest.

The tracks were hard-packed and frozen, making travelling relatively easy. I rode all day, stopping only to feed my horse and cut more lines, hampering communications even further. It gave me great pleasure to carry out this sabotage. I saw it as paying the Soviet system back for all the misery it had made me suffer in this Siberian hell-hole. I knew it would take them several weeks to repair the lines and by then, with luck, I would be a thousand miles away.

At twenty-mile intervals there were the usual barracks, erected to provide shelter for travellers. I used them to my advantage, snuggling up to my horse for warmth and protection through the night. I stopped at each village, hurriedly checking a couple of lines and explaining that there was a serious fault and I was having difficulty tracing it. I was left alone to continue my work and I travelled without incident. I was averaging forty miles per day, which was good considering the conditions, which were worsening. The drifts were higher and I wasted time picking my way through the deep snow.

I re-checked my map. I reckoned I had roughly 45 miles to go and approximately 15 to the next barracks. It was growing dusk and the forests came alive at night. I knew it wasn't safe to stop, so I spurred my horse on, hoping to reach shelter before nightfall. The lack of a moon made matters worse.

Suddenly my horse stopped, his ears pricked. He refused to move. I peered into the gloom but could see nothing. We moved off the track, picking our way round the outer edges of the forest. Again he stopped and this time I heard a rustling noise. I stood up in the saddle trying to pick out movement. Another rustle, this time behind me. These were the sounds of wolves and a sudden blood-curdling howl confirmed it.

The horse became restless, snorting and moving around in a tight circle. My instincts were to move fast but he remained rooted to the spot. I had to decide quickly what to do if I was to save myself. I dismounted hurriedly, unsaddled the horse and, using my whip, spurred him to run into the forest to safety. But he wouldn't go. He had always been a faithful friend and now he stood watching me with his big soulful eyes, not understanding and seemingly unaware that I was trying to help him survive.

Making one last desperate attempt to move him, I slapped his buttocks, swearing and cursing at him the whole time, but he remained stubbornly immovable. At the same time the smell of the wolves became stronger as they homed in on our scent. I could wait no longer. Fixing my climbing hooks on to my boots, I began to shin up the highest tree. I stopped, hoping my absence would bring him to his senses but he simply stood and watched me, wanting my help. But I couldn't help him anymore, he could only help himself. If I'd had a rifle, one shot would have sufficed to drive the wolves off. As it was, I was totally helpless.

When the wolves came into view it was clear that they had encircled us. I felt bile rising in my throat. Why did he stay? In desperation I shouted to him.

'Go! Go! You stupid animal! Can't you see I'm trying to save you?! For God's sake, run!' The wolves hesitated at the sound of my voice but fear oozed from the horse's body and fear was an element that the wolves thrived on. I carried on shouting but my voice was becoming hoarse and eventually the wolves ignored me. Now at last he moved, kicking out at the scrawny wolves, suddenly realising that he had made the biggest mistake of his life. The grey, shaggy, furred animals approached closer and closer, baring their teeth and howling at the scent of blood.

One brave wolf attacked and the horse kicked out, throwing his attacker into the air. The wolf howled in pain, his pride hurt. He came back for the attack, this time aiming for the horse's neck, sharp teeth tearing into his flesh. The other wolves, smelling the blood, followed. Within seconds they were tearing him to pieces, attacking each other as well in their fight for food. The bile rose and I vomited unashamedly at the horrific sight beneath me.

I struggled to stay in the tree, my body becoming numb. Since I had no means of escape, I cautiously edged my way further up the trunk until I was wedged into the 'V' of the trunk and the strongest bough. Sensing the movement, half a dozen of the wolves surrounded the tree. I had no intention of becoming their dessert, so I dug my climbing hooks firmly into the trunk. Two of the braver wolves leapt at the tree baring their teeth. As their claws ripped the tree bark, they howled in frustration. It was obvious that I was too high and eventually they grew tired of their game, going back to the half-eaten carcass.

I tried to shelter myself from the cold as well as I could, covering my face with the warm coat and pulling my sleeves over my hands. When the cold became unbearable I scolded myself.

'You've grown soft; after all you've suffered much worse conditions than these. Pull yourself together! You didn't take all the risks of escape merely to become a meal for wolves.'

Dawn eventually arrived. The frost was at its keenest and I felt as if rigor mortis had set in when I tried to move my limbs. The wolves had been resting after their sumptuous meal but as dawn broke, their leader, sensing that it was time to leave, stood up, circled the tree and looked at me menacingly as if to confirm that he would be back. Then, with the briskness of a company commander, he turned and headed into the forest, his patrol following in his footsteps. The howling grew fainter but I was very wary as I struggled to climb down the tree. My circulation seemed to have stopped. I had to hold on to the tree trunk for support as I stamped feeling back into my feet. Eventually pins and needles attacked my limbs as the circulation began to flow.

Retrieving my saddle, I delved into the bag for the remains of my provisions, two slices of dried bread, one of which I ate. I washed this down with a handful of virgin snow. Another handful was used to freshen up my face, making the skin tingle and tighten. I then emptied the tools out of my bags and strapped them on my back. The long, tedious journey on foot following the telephone lines began. I planned to cover the last 40 miles to Sosnogorsk in the next couple of days.

I desperately needed to reach shelter by nightfall, especially since it had started snowing heavily and the conditions were getting worse by the hour, with the freezing Siberian winds whipping up the snow in exposed areas. What spurred me on was the vision of my horse's carcass and the menacing look of the pack leader as he led his army back into the forest. My one consolation was that if a search party was following my tracks, they would find my saddle and the remains of my horse and conclude that I too had perished.

# Chapter Fifteen

# *A Continuing Journey*

As I trudged through the snow, I felt sad and depressed at the death of my best, most loyal friend. The nightmare of his end kept returning to haunt me and I could not eradicate the image of those two soulful eyes staring up at me in desperation.

To add to my problems, the provisions I'd brought with me were exhausted and all I had left were two packets of tobacco, a small amount of money and my working tools. I dreaded nightfall, knowing what easy prey I'd be for the wolves. Reviewing my position, I estimated I'd walked about five miles but still had ten miles to go before reaching the next barracks. Though my situation seemed hopeless, I redoubled my efforts to try to gain shelter before dark.

Suddenly, in the total silence, I heard a voice shouting.

'*Paganiaj! Paganiaj!*'

Looking round, I saw a sledge about to overtake me and stepped aside into the deep snow to let it pass. The driver, a Russian hunter, was obviously in a great hurry, but he seemed so surprised to see a lone traveller on foot that he reined his horses to a halt. Looking me up and down and noting my warm clothing and tools, he seemed satisfied that I had a legitimate occupation.

'What happened to your horse and rifle?' he asked, out of curiosity rather than suspicion.

I told him about the wolves, adding that my rifle had jammed at the crucial moment and I'd been unable to shoot. Since it was no longer any use, I'd discarded it along the way. I made out that I had to get to Sosnogorsk as quickly as possible to repair a major telephone fault in the town.

Accepting this story without further ado, he allowed me a ride on his sledge to Sosnogorsk. What a relief! I gratefully accepted and settled down between the hay and the thick fur pelts. When he asked me if I had any tobacco, I was naturally delighted to share some with him, and hastily rolled two cigarettes, one for each of us. He smoked his to the very end, almost burning his lips as he took a final puff. When he'd finished he explained why he too was making for Sosnogorsk. In his settlement there'd been no deliveries of food and provisions for over a month. Hence the load of pelts on the sledge, which he intended to exchange for food and tobacco.

Fingering the soft pelts, I felt something hard underneath them. Moving them ever so slightly, I caught sight of my saddle. I tried to pretend I hadn't seen it since I didn't want to alarm him and I was, after all, very grateful for the lift. But my movement had not escaped him and a look of panic crossed his face. He quickly decided that honesty was the best policy.

'I found that saddle near your horse's skeleton. Take it back if you want. I just thought it'd help me get extra provisions. It's a good saddle and worth quite a lot on the black market.'

I shrugged.

'Keep it. I'm grateful for the ride and anyway I expect I'll be given a new horse and saddle for the journey back. But I tell you what I should like – a large hunting knife, if you've got one, for protection against the wolves.'

I knew he'd have one and, to do him justice, he was more than ready to give it to me. The prospect of having a knife made me a little more confident about the next stage of my journey and I settled down to rest, feeling quite safe in the company of this new companion.

But when we began to approach the town, I realised that I might be in some danger. If he took me straight to NKVD headquarters, which would be the normal thing to do, I should almost certainly be arrested and that would be the end of my escape attempt. My mind was working overtime. Suddenly I had an idea and asked him to stop.

'We don't want the NKVD to know about the saddle,' I said. 'If you make it public that you've given me a lift and they find out about the saddle we'll both be in serious trouble. Drop me off here and I'll walk into town. I'll tell my story and you can sell the saddle with no questions asked.'

Evidently seeing the sense in what I'd said, he grinned, showing his black, stunted teeth.

'You're right. Here's the knife I promised you. It's very sharp so you can kill a wolf with one blow, providing you strike it in the right place.'

He showed me how to do it. In return I gave him what was left of my packet of tobacco. His eyes sparkled as he took it from me.

It was dusk as I entered the outskirts of the town. I was now among normal everyday people. It was up to me to use my brain, keep calm and not panic. With a bit of luck I should be on a train next day out of this northern nightmare.

I found overnight shelter in a makeshift hut but was up at first light. I wandered round the town. Militia, NKVD, soldiers and civilians intermingled and the atmosphere was quite relaxed. Nobody was interested in me. Yet I felt extremely nervous in this novel situation.

When the stores opened, I bought tobacco and smoked cigarette after cigarette to combat my nervousness. My stomach rumbled and my throat was dry with the cigarette smoke. Eventually I came across a huge cooperative coffee house. I watched and waited as both civilians and soldiers entered the building. It was time to take a chance. The room was divided into two sections, one for civilians and the other for soldiers and officials. I joined the civilian queue which, by that time, was quite lengthy. Suddenly I felt a hand on my shoulder. My blood froze. I immediately thought my sabotage had been discovered and I was being arrested. Turning, I looked straight into the eyes of an NKVD man. To my amazement he released me and beckoned me to follow him. This was my only chance. Did I attack him from behind and make a run for it? I repeated over and over again to myself, 'Keep calm, keep calm.'

Again I was surprised. He took me to the front of the queue and announced:

'This man has work to do. He can't waste his precious time standing in this queue so give him what he wants.'

No one objected as I was served with hot coffee, a double portion of bread and butter and two eggs. There'd been no objections because, as I'd observed on other occasions, all Soviet authority was based on breaking established rules. The people who reached the top fastest were the profoundest liars and the cruellest officials. Generally, civilians let them show their authority in order to have a quiet life.

Since my luck seemed to be in, I decided to take my food with me and make for the railway station, hoping to find an empty cattle truck or something similar heading south. I walked up and down the platform trying to avoid suspicion. But not one train had a southern destination. The sidings were my last chance. Here the wagons were loaded, coupled up and left standing until a locomotive was available.

Eventually I found a heavy goods train, destination Kirov, obviously fully loaded as the locomotive was already coupled up to it, which meant it would be moving that day. I hastily searched the wagons and found one containing large wooden crates and a certain amount of straw. I carefully slid the door back and climbed in, closing it behind me, but leaving a slight gap until my eyes became accustomed to the semi-darkness. So far, so good.

A rustling noise made me jump. Rats, I thought. But there it was again, coming from behind the cases. I stood with my back to the door, eyes darting from packing case to packing case. Suddenly a man appeared, his knife gleaming in the ray of light coming from the gap in the doorway. In the semi-darkness he looked like someone possessed. Ragged clothes covered his emaciated body. There was hatred in his eyes. And he was not alone, to judge from other rustling noises coming from behind the cases. My own knife was tucked safely in my belt and I fingered it, hoping to use it at the last minute, thus surprising my assailant. I composed myself, thinking about my army training. I would have only one chance. How many friends had he behind the cases?

Suddenly he lunged forward. I dodged the knife and hit him in the face. He staggered backwards, recovered and attacked again. I pulled out my knife and aimed for his right arm, slashing him just above the elbow. The sudden pain caused him to drop his own knife in surprise. I kicked it out of reach. Two equally bedraggled specimens then appeared from behind the cases. Acting quickly I kicked the nearest assailant in the groin sending him spinning into the corner. The third man, not wanting the same treatment, stayed in the background, knife in hand. The first attacker was once again advancing towards me. I ducked, grabbing his body as he tackled me. For one awful moment, I felt vulnerable but his two companions were slow. Managing to turn my assailant, I pressed my knife to his throat and turned to face the other two.

By threatening to kill him, I succeeded in persuading his friends to drop their knives. Once in control I had the chance to tell them I wasn't an official but a prisoner on the run, as I assumed they were. I warned them not to make any more noise if they wanted to escape recapture. Releasing the pressure on my assailant's throat, I waited for a counter-attack. But he seemed now to have relaxed. I told them I'd come from Pechora Camp and didn't want to risk being caught but I felt there was enough room for all of us in the wagon. What's more I could be useful to them and they should think about that.

I rolled four cigarettes, keeping my knife within snatching distance. Taking the cigarettes, they inhaled deeply. They told me their names were Igor, Vanka and Volodia. They had all three worked on the railway link-up to Vorkuta, where conditions had been as appalling as in Pechora and large numbers had died of starvation, frostbite, gangrene and cruelty. They had travelled for a week, finding the wagons under cover of darkness. It was obvious they couldn't go into town to scrounge food since their appearance would have given them away immediately.

I produced a loaf of bread and tossed it to them. They tore it apart, almost choking in the effort of swallowing. They shook their heads and laughed when I asked if they had any money. They became quite friendly, apart from Igor who resented me, resented my warm clothes and my efficiency. I knew that if I ever turned my back on him I could expect a knife between my shoulder blades. Eventually he put his hand in his pocket. I waited for another knife to appear but instead he offered me five roubles, the grand total of their wealth. Even though it would not buy much I took it as a matter of principle. I had to remain in charge. I left them, saying I would return with more bread before the train left.

The queues for supplies were now rather long. It was early afternoon and the streets were teeming with people. Not knowing how much time I had before the train left, I plucked up courage and went to the front of one of the queues, where I asked for four loaves of bread. The shop assistant looked me up and down and people in the queue swore. She beckoned to a militia man who was keeping an eye on the queue. As he approached I felt my blood drain but managed to remain calm as he politely asked me why I'd gone to the front. I explained that my workmates and I had identified the serious telephone fault that had interrupted all communications with Troitsko Pechorsk. We hoped to get at least one line working before nightfall but since the problem was five miles out of town, we wouldn't be able to return to Sosnogorsk before dusk and by then it would be too late to buy food.

He scrutinised my clothes, my tools and the handset that I blatantly displayed on my belt. Then, slowly taking out his notebook and a roll of food tickets, he scribbled something in the book, tore off four food tickets, signed them and handed them to the assistant. In turn she gave me four loaves of bread, free of charge. Thanking him profusely I assured him, in my most ingratiating manner, that I would report to my superiors at Troitsko Pechorsk how helpful he'd been. I left the store unhurriedly, detoured round the outskirts of the town and approached the station from the opposite direction.

It suddenly occurred to me that we needed water for the

journey. I scoured the sidings for a receptacle, eventually finding a dented old bucket which I hastened to fill with tap water before making my way back to the train. My fellow fugitives were surprised to see me, assuming I wouldn't return, and even more surprised to see the bread and water on which they pounced greedily. I stopped them eating everything at once since we didn't know where our next meal would come from. I settled myself in a corner making sure my provisions were safe and my knife near to hand. Slowly the train began to move out of the station. I breathed a huge sigh of relief since every mile was a mile further away from Pechora Camp and certain death.

The gentle movement of the train relaxed me and thoughts began to rush through my brain. I'd managed to travel so far undetected, but now I had a millstone around my neck. Surely I'd made a terrible mistake coming back to the wagon. Wouldn't it have been better to find another one where I could be on my own and meditate on my journey, preparing myself for what might come next? I couldn't totally relax with these three prisoners, who confessed that they weren't political prisoners at all but common thieves. I was convinced that Igor would kill me for my warm clothes and provisions if given half a chance.

I decided to give him that chance. Nestling in the straw, I pretended to be asleep while listening for the slightest sound or movement. Though his friends were asleep, Igor was restless. He thought I was asleep too. Stealthily he moved forward, hesitating slightly. I could smell his stale breath as he bent over me and I could picture the knife ready to strike. I moved fast as lightning and caught him totally unawares, striking his leg with my knife.

Dropping his own knife, he clutched his leg in pain. His companions were roused by the noise and jumped to their feet. For one awful moment I thought they were about to defend their leader, but when they realised what had happened they swore at Igor and went back to sleep.

'You'd better not try a third time,' I warned him. 'Your arm, your leg, next time your heart!'

I picked up the discarded knife, throwing it out of the door into the thickening snow. He retired to his corner like a wounded dog, ripping his already tattered shirt to make a bandage for his wounded leg. This time I fell into a deep sleep knowing that his courage wouldn't allow him to try again.

'KOTLAS'. The name stood out in bold letters as the train slowed to a halt. It was time for me to fetch fresh supplies of food and water. I secretly hoped that the train would pull out of the station before my return, relieving me of the millstone of my companions. I again joined the queue for bread, surprised to see civilians, militia and soldiers all mingling together. There could be no queue-jumping this time. In front of me was a broad, rough-looking man dressed rather like myself, with a newspaper sticking out of his overcoat pocket. I ventured to ask him for the latest news, pointing to the newspaper.

'For one rouble it's yours,' he replied. 'I got it the same way.' I gave him a rouble and he handed me the paper. Turning his back on me, he made it obvious he didn't want any more conversation. Various pieces of information from the paper stuck in my mind. German soldiers were within striking distance of Moscow. Thousands of factory workers had joined the People's Volunteer Force which, together with the Soviet army, was defending the city of Leningrad. Two million members of the Komsomol, the League of Communist Youth, had been conscripted. There was an article on evacuation which reported that ten million people had been relocated in the Urals, Kazakhstan and other Central Asian republics. Kiev had fallen to German troops on 19 September, Odessa on 16 October. I digested as much information as I could since I wanted to avoid areas which might be controlled by German troops.

The queue moved slowly since each person was closely scrutinised by NKVD personnel before the bread ration was handed over. I decided to use the same story I'd used in Sosnogorsk, that I and my three colleagues were repairing a major fault just outside Kotlas. However, when I eventually reached the end of the queue and came under scrutiny, my courage failed me and I received the statutory one loaf of bread.

I detoured once more but the station was a hive of activity and I was totally ignored as I refilled my bucket and slipped between the carriages back to the truck. My companions groaned as I produced the solitary loaf. I could contain my anger no longer, forcefully pointing out that I was risking my life to feed them and without me they'd be dead.

As I turned away in disgust, the train began to pull out of the station. Pulling the newspaper out of my pocket, I managed to re-read some of the main stories, my eyes straining in the semidarkness. Thankfully the train to Kirov was fast, stopping only occasionally at the smaller stations along the line. The journey passed without incident.

Kirov was an extremely busy station on the main line from Moscow and Gorki to Perm and Vladivostok. I wandered through the sidings, bucket in hand, trying not to arouse suspicion as I checked each destination plate. There were many trains but none seemed to be going in the right direction. I had hoped to get a train to Kazan which would take me towards my ultimate destination of Orsk and Tashkent. Most of the trains, though, seemed to be going in the opposite direction, to Gorki and Moscow. Hiding my bucket, I decided to search the main station in the hope of finding a loaf of bread. I wasn't sure how long I could keep up the pretence of repairing telephone faults. Sooner or later I was bound to be asked for my identification.

The platforms were heavy with people and, to my horror, I realised they were all prisoners waiting for transport to the labour camps in the familiar boarded-up trucks. I shuddered as soldiers prodded and kicked the half-starved prisoners as they stumbled down the platform, remembering only too vividly my own horrific journey. This sight certainly unnerved me and I didn't have the courage to queue for bread, fearing detection and a fate like that of the prisoners. Turning away from the distressing scene, I made my way back to the sidings and relative safety.

Since I'd left, another train had pulled into the sidings and, to my relief, I found it was going to Perm. Doing a hasty check I found four cattle trucks at the end of the train. Three of them were padlocked but the fourth was open. From the stench it appeared they'd been used fairly recently. Inside, the straw was well trodden with cattle dung. Since it was almost dusk, I couldn't risk being caught wandering around the sidings so I decided that this was the best I was likely to get.

Suddenly I remembered the water, which I couldn't do without. Making sure the coast was clear, I set off to retrieve my bucket, nervously filling it at the communal tap. When I returned it was almost dark. As I fumbled with the doors, I became aware of rustling noises close by.

Turning, I saw three shadowy figures running across the lines towards me. It was obvious that I hadn't managed to escape from my three companions after all.

They jumped into the truck. Initially recoiling at the stench, they quickly recovered and started looking around for food, obviously without success. I settled down in my corner, making it quite obvious that I'd no wish to talk. During the night the train pulled out. Luckily it was another fast journey. As we picked up speed, the fresh air rushing in through the partially closed door brought relief from the stench and I managed to sleep propped up in the corner, lulled by the motion of the train.

During the following day the train stopped several times but it was unsafe to leave the truck. The smaller stations were quieter, with only the occasional railway employee or soldier on the platform. I was continually harassed by my companions, who complained incessantly of their hunger. I became deeply depressed as the cold, hunger and fatigue took their toll. When we finally arrived at Perm, the train pulled into one of the main platforms. I could hear the echoing footsteps of the guards as they walked up and down. Doors opened and shut. My heart was in my mouth. I remained motionless and silent in my corner, trying to blend into the background. Soon all the banging and activity on the platform stopped. The train began to go backwards and then forwards, stopping each time with a jolt. We were obviously being shunted into a siding. Eventually we shuddered to a halt. It seemed we were in line to be loaded the following day.

It was two hours before I dared venture out. As we expected, our four trucks had been shunted into a siding along with many others. I crept along the line, finding it difficult to read the destination plates in the darkness of the moonless night. I hoped to find better accommodation, but above all I wanted to shake off my travelling companions. On the track nearest to the station stood a line of brand-new wagons. I examined them cautiously, looking for the destination plate without success. The doors were padlocked. A notice was fastened to the door of the last truck, which I read with difficulty.

'PROVISIONS, AUTHORISED PERSONNEL ONLY.'

Having had nothing to eat for three days, I felt my taste buds beginning to work overtime. Here was a truckful of food and all that was in the way was a huge padlock. It was time for my companions to make themselves useful. As professional thieves, they should find breaking into the wagon child's play. Going back to our truck, I briefed the experts. They followed me to the wagon and I left them to their work while continuing my search for a new truck.

Eventually I found a train going to Sverdlovsk. Its trucks were cleaner and rough benches had been nailed to the walls. Leaving the door ajar, I returned to the provisions truck, not trusting my companions. I discovered that they had already broken in and were hurriedly filling new buckets with tobacco, sausage, ham, bread and chocolate. There was even a case of vodka. I showed them to our new home. We emptied the buckets and returned for more. I sorted the food into four equal shares, helping myself freely to extra ham and sausage.

When they returned with buckets filled to the brim, they assured me that they had refastened the door and covered their tracks, leaving no sign whatsoever of entry. True professionals!

I'd no reason to disbelieve them and, anyway, I was eager to eat my fill. I'd no intention of checking for myself. We closed the door, gorging ourselves on the food and doing justice to the vodka. Once our hunger was satisfied, we settled down on the rough benches and pretty soon fell into a drunken sleep.

# Chapter Sixteen

## *Execution*

Soviet army guards were very careful about their supplies of food and rations and made frequent checks. Given the conditions of extreme scarcity after war broke out, pilfering was to be expected, but it was subject to severe punishment. Sometimes the guards themselves were unable to resist temptation. They, like any other culprits, could expect deportation to the camps if they were found out.

Now, standing in front of the supply wagon, the soldiers were horrified. Broken locks and splinters of wood littered the snow. Inside, boxes and packages had been torn apart. No attempt had been made to conceal the crime; even fresh footprints in the snow were plainly visible. The lieutenant's initial dismay quickly disappeared when he saw that arresting the culprits would be an easy task.

In my drunken sleep I was totally unaware of what was going on outside. Somewhere in my subconscious, I became aware of the wagon doors opening, voices drifting on the wind, daylight flooding my eyes. I tried to focus on the uniforms. Six, I counted, four soldiers, one corporal, one lieutenant. Their bodies seemed to merge into one since my eyes, still heavy with drink, wouldn't stay in focus. I was vaguely aware of the lieutenant accusing us of theft; there could be no doubt about it, we'd been caught with the spoils of our crime. Igor's face confirmed our guilt, he shouted: more scars on his face than the station had railway lines! There was only one punishment for people like us: shooting. A bullet through the head was all we deserved. We were the dregs of society and didn't have the right to live. He was obviously leading up to ordering our immediate execution when he was interrupted by his corporal.

'We can't shoot them here in the wagon, sir. There'll be too much noise and the train'll be held up while the NKVD investigates. Perhaps we should take them to the inspection sheds.'

The lieutenant saw the sense of this but told his men to hurry up since the train was on the point of leaving. I have a vivid image of him pacing up and down impatiently and continually striking his left hand with his gloves.

I slowly began to realise what a desperate situation I was in. But before I could even begin to think of a way out, one of the soldiers prodded me with his bayonet as I lay on the floor of the wagon, manhandled me to my feet and shoved me roughly out of the door. I landed face down in the snow. My accomplices followed me one by one, their legs not strong enough to support them, their eyes still heavy with drink. We were frogmarched towards the inspection building, the soldiers prodding and pushing the whole time.

The fresh air brought me to my senses. I couldn't believe that this was really happening to me. I had been so careful. One mistake! Why hadn't I checked the supply wagon? Instead I'd acted like an idiot, drinking and eating myself into a state of oblivion. Had I suffered all these years for nothing, enduring the traumas of escape only to be shot with a trio of common thieves? I prayed as I stumbled across the rough ground, offering my soul to God who had given me so many chances, and begging forgiveness for my many sins.

The shrill whistle of the supply train interrupted my prayers. For a brief moment the corporal hesitated and looked back but was quickly reassured by a signal from the lieutenant that the train was not leaving without them. The soldiers resumed their prodding and pushing. My legs were like rubber and my bladder felt weak. I'd been in similar situations in Pechora Lager but never before had I felt such intense fear. I gabbled a consoling prayer, commending my soul to God.

The shots rang out, one, two, three. I waited for the fourth bullet, aware of the gun pointing at me. The Lord's Prayer was on my lips as the fourth shot sent me crashing to the ground, the echo reverberating through my skull, numbing my brain. A searing pain flashed coloured strands across my eyes and my head felt as if a heavy hammer had dealt its fatal blow before I slipped into deep unconsciousness. In my unconscious state, I was aware of a voice fighting to be heard. 'It isn't over yet.' The words span round and round in my head. 'It isn't over yet.'

I drifted on the edge of consciousness unaware of my surroundings, sensitive only to the numbing coldness of my limbs and the throbbing pain in my head. My eyes wouldn't focus and it was a relief to slip back into unconsciousness. In my mind I was gliding across the snow on a pure white sledge, pulled by pure white horses. I was moving faster and faster, the falling snow stinging my cheeks. I opened my eyes. Someone was dragging me across the snow. Two pairs of black boots stood out against the whiteness. I wanted to shout that I was alive, to ask where they were taking me. But my lips wouldn't from the words and my mind went blank. Through my blurred vision, I could see someone digging. I made out the figures of a man and woman, the man dressed in some sort of uniform, the woman in a peasant skirt and shawl. Why were they digging holes in the frozen ground? I moved my head sideways, wincing at the blinding pain. When my eyes re-focused, I saw the body of Igor, his scars standing out like ridges on his ashen face. The pain increased and I slipped back into oblivion.

Now, in my dreams, I was back in Pechora Camp. I'd been shot, I couldn't communicate, I was being buried alive! But this was no dream, this was reality! My whole life flashed before my eyes: my mother and father holding out their arms to hug me in my childhood; the strict life behind the walls of the Jesuit college; my days in the army; Pechora Lager; the train journey and now, the stark reality, the bullet. As consciousness returned I tried to speak. A moan escaped my lips. The effort was unbearable.

Now I was moving across the snow again. Someone was

gripping my hands. I saw the perimeter of a large hole, the bodies of my companions already placed side by side. 'No! No! Oh my God, help me!' The words escaped as the pressure closed in, sending me into unconsciousness once more.

The woman stood on the edge of the grave staring at me, not knowing what to do. I knew I'd got to make one last effort to communicate. I opened my eyes, turning my head to face her. She dropped to her knees making the sign of the cross and shouting to the man.

'Dimitriev, Dimitriev, he's alive, he's alive!'

The pain in my bead was blinding. The effort had been too much but I was aware of someone touching me, loosening my clothes. How close was I to death? Were they helping me or robbing me? I opened my eyes again. The woman was still kneeling by my side, the man standing behind her. I began to recite the Lord's Prayer, miming most of the words.

'Our Father, who art in heaven, hallowed be thy name.'

The man fell to his knees clasping his hands, and, for several minutes, they joined me in prayer, signing me with the Sign of the Cross when we had finished.

Now they were bending over me, examining my wound. I learned later that the bullet had caught my earlobe, entered my neck, passed through the neck muscles close to the top of my spine and had come out on the opposite side. Fortunately the corporal had been in a hurry and had aimed too low, so my brain was uninjured. It was the tremendous shock to my nervous system that caused the pain and lack of co-ordination. Unconsciousness was a blessing. As I drifted into the darkness once more, I asked God to take me, or give me back the strength to resume my journey.

I wasn't sure how long I remained unconscious. When I came to, the smell of fresh hay filled my nostrils. Though my head ached, the searing pain had gone. I still felt terribly weak, even the effort of moving my arm to my bandaged neck was exhausting. But by some miracle I was still alive.

Dimitriev and Irena were of Russian peasant stock. They both worked on the railway. He was in charge of a ten-mile stretch of line, his chief task being to keep it clear of any obstruction, particularly snowdrifts. His wife worked on the station, cleaning the platforms and waiting rooms. They were a deeply religious couple. Not being permitted to practise their faith openly, they had turned their secret cellar into a shrine and their Sunday mornings were spent in prayer before their icon. They had tended my wounds every day. I'd lived in a twilight zone for almost a week but now they rejoiced in prayer as I opened my eyes and moved my arm.

They'd hidden me in the hay store, a tiny annex at the side of the single stable, used solely for the storage of hay and straw. They feared reprisals since harbouring a prisoner was a serious offence, often punishable by death. However, officialdom didn't seem to intrude on their lives very much and as long as they worked hard there was no reason for the militia or railway supervisors to come out to visit them.

Now, as my strength began to return, they offered me a bed in their humble home. In case of emergency I was to go down into the cellar, the entrance to which was a trapdoor behind the house, covered in straw. I was to stay there as long as necessary.

I owe Dimitriev and Irena my life. If they had not, out of compassion, decided to bury the four bodies they had stumbled over on their way to work, I would have died. They told me how they'd waited until after nightfall to carry me back to their house, not having the courage to move me in broad daylight. They'd hoped I'd survive the cold. Now, under their care, I was slowly on the mend. They couldn't have treated their own son with greater kindness and love. Over the next few months they became my dear friends. During the dark, cold nights I told them my life story, everything from my childhood to the day they'd found me.

In return they told me about themselves and the cause of their present sadness. They had a son, Yuri, who had also worked on the railway, travelling all over the country as a ticket inspector on passenger trains. He'd had plenty of friends and enjoyed a good social life. One of these friends, Alexander, was a signalman who'd lived alone with his mother until some NKVD men burst into their home and arrested his mother for some trivial offence. She never returned. To overcome his loneliness and his hatred of the authorities, he used to invite his friends to his home where there was plenty of food and the vodka flowed freely.

At one of these parties, matters got out of hand. Alexander got drunk and set out to gain some sort of revenge for his mother's arrest. He staggered towards the square, determined to violate the Soviet flag. His friends, Yuri among them, tried to stop him but he was like a man possessed. Finding the flag he spat on it vehemently. He'd have torn it apart if his friends hadn't restrained him. They took him home. They'd all been lucky to escape arrest since a curfew operated during the hours of darkness.

However, Vladimir, another friend, had witnessed this 'violation' of the flag. An ordinary railway worker himself, he reported the incident to the NKVD in the hope of promotion. Consequently Alexander was arrested. For his counter-revolutionary behaviour and his desecration of the Soviet flag, he was shot. Yuri, though taking no active part in the crime, was sentenced to ten years' hard labour in the Kolyma gold mines for failing to report the incident and for helping Alexander to the safety of his home. Vladimir was rewarded by promotion to station master but was sent to a desolate place deep in the Siberian forests, never to be seen again.

No word had been received from Yuri since that fateful day when the train full of prisoners had pulled out of the railway station. I shuddered as I thought about the horrific stories I'd told Dimitriev and Irena about life in the labour camps which they seemed to know nothing about. I tried to console them. Perhaps, I reflected, conditions in the gold mines were not as arduous as in the camps. Perhaps Yuri would return to them as soon as the war was over.

I started to think about resuming my journey. I began my preparations by changing my appearance. The beard that I'd worn for so many years disappeared. I had my hair cut in a style that seemed to be favoured by many Russian men. I had been lucky with my clothing. Normally bodies were stripped naked after a shooting since clothing could be reused and strict orders were in force to return all garments to headquarters. But the soldiers had been in a hurry, not wanting to attract attention to themselves, nor to hold up the train. They hadn't even checked to see if we were dead. So I still had my thick warm coat and fur-lined boots. Alas, my telephone equipment had been left behind in the wagon when I was captured.

By the beginning of March 1942 my strength had returned, and the wound in my neck had healed perfectly, thanks to the tender love and care of Dimitriev and Irena. I did not wish to outstay my welcome but neither did I want to leave. Though truly grateful to them for their hospitality, I had to start planning the next part of my escape. Having lost my telephone equipment, I had to assume another identity to enable me to travel without suspicion. Dimitriev and Irena were devastated when I told them I was leaving. To them I was like a son. Irena secretly wished I would stay forever, though she knew it was impossible. They pleaded with me to stay one more month until spring brought a slow thaw but I wouldn't commit myself, saying that as soon as I felt the time was right I'd leave.

I spent part of each day reading the newspapers which Irena found in the station rooms and brought home daily, tucked out of sight under her shawl. I studied the international news and the reports of the German advance deep into the Soviet Union. It seemed that two thirds of the German army was concentrated on the Russian front and was now advancing towards Stalingrad. Apparently the Germans were planning to cross the River Don to strengthen their position.

I also learned that General Sikorski, the Prime Minister of the Polish Government-in-Exile in London, had signed an agreement with Stalin to form a Polish army inside the Soviet Union. There were one and a half million Polish deportees in Siberia alone.

121

Special permits were issued to them so they could travel to join the Polish army. Ultimately many seized the opportunity to leave the Soviet Union by way of Persia. However, I knew I wouldn't qualify for such a pass, having been found guilty of spying. My escape from Pechora Camp simply compounded my crime. I had no alternative but to remain on the run. Yet the news that some Polish units were also in Persia and Palestine made me feel a little happier and I threw all my energy into planning the next stage of my journey to freedom.

# Chapter Seventeen

## *Sad Farewell*

As the snow melted, rich tufts of green began to show through the white blanket. Buds burst into life. Spring was arriving and with it the urge to resume my arduous journey. Feeling physically and mentally fit, thanks to the loving care of my Russian friends, I could delay my departure no longer. I told them of my plans, though with some sadness, since I knew how much they wanted me to stay.

I felt my best chance of escape was to cross the border into Afghanistan. But the distance from Perm to Samarkand was 2,000 miles; it was plainly out of the question to try to walk that far. To travel by train I would need some cover since my warm clothes would mean nothing without the telephone equipment snapped round my waist. I knew that Dimitriev and Irena still kept their son's railway uniform in their little chapel. I explained my travel plans to them and hoped they'd offer the uniform spontaneously. But, as my day of departure approached, they still hadn't referred to it and I couldn't pluck up the courage to ask them. It looked as though my hopes would be dashed.

Soon it was the eve of my departure and I knew that if I was to obtain the uniform, I should have to seize the moment. I was under no illusions as to how painful it would be for this gentle couple, who had done so much for me already, to part with their most precious possession in order to help me escape. Nevertheless, that evening I went to them, took their hands and kissed them as a son kisses his parents before setting off on a journey. When I spoke my voice trembled with emotion.

'I know it's too much to ask. You've treated me like a son, feeding me and protecting me. I owe you my life. But I have one more request to make of you. I desperately need a uniform to help me travel on the trains without suspicion. I know your son's uniform is your most cherished possession, but you know as well as I do that I can't escape without it. I really need your help yet again.'

Dimitriev put his head in his hands and tears escaped between his fingers. Irena watched him silently, a look of deep misery etched on her face. When, finally, he lifted his tear-stained face his eyes reflected his deep sorrow. His words were an answer to my prayers.

'The uniform is yours, even though I'll be cutting the last remaining link with our son. But I shall pray for his freedom every day just as I also pray for yours. But I beg you to take care. If you're arrested, our lives will be in danger and we're too old to spend the rest of our days in a labour camp.'

I solemnly promised that their lives were safe with me and if I was arrested I'd rather take my own life than implicate them. I assured them that I loved them as much as I loved my own parents.

Irena then led the way through the trapdoor and into the chapel. Lovingly she fingered the rough uniform for the last time, her tears falling on the cloth. Suddenly she urged me to try it on to make sure it fitted. Hastily I stripped and pulled on the trousers, fastening the belt. The jacket was a perfect fit, only the trousers were a shade too long.

'I'll shorten them for you, but first I must give you something else.'

She crossed the room to a small closet and took out a black bag of the kind carried by railway employees at the stations. Inside the bag was a ticket punch, various bits and pieces and a set of identity papers permitting a railway inspector to travel the country. I hugged Irena and the tears flowed. I'd just lived through one of the most emotional days of my life.

That night, sleep was fitful. My mind was alert as I relived the events of that evening. I got up at dawn and put on Yuri's uniform. I was apprehensive of the inevitable farewells. My friends were waiting to say goodbye and the air was charged with emotion as we embraced. Dimitriev took my hand.

'Here, take this, it's all I have but you're welcome to it.'

He pressed some money into the palm of my hand. When I protested, he silenced me.

'I hope there's someone, somewhere, helping my son as I'm helping you. God bless you, Misha. Good luck on your journey. I shall pray for you.'

He turned away, holding his head in his hands, sobbing uncontrollably. Irena comforted him.

'Don't upset yourself, Dimitriev. Misha is a second son to us. Look, he's survived the camps and Yuri too will survive and come back to us.'

Dimitriev composed himself and putting his hands on my shoulders he made his prophecy.

'I know you'll survive. You'll be a free man. We shall meet again, if not in this world then in the next. I shall pray for you, please pray for me.'

Sobbing, I held him to me.

'Thank you from my heart. Thank you for saving my life, thank you for your love and your hospitality and for this uniform. If there is a God, as we believe, He will help us. One day things will improve and Yuri will return to you.'

I said my last goodbyes and received their last blessing. As I set off towards the station, I knew that they stood watching my every step as I slowly disappeared from their lives for ever. It's so hard for me to express my feelings for this Russian couple. My love for them will remain with me for the rest of my life. The contrast was complete. On one side a lonely mother and father who had lost their totally innocent son to a labour camp and who had saved, loved and protected a complete stranger with as much love as they had lavished on their boy. On the other, the ruthless Communist government led by the sadistic Stalin who gave a damn for nobody and trampled over everyone in his lust for supreme power.

Waiting on that bleak station platform, I pulled myself together. Irena told me that the early morning train was going to Chelyabinsk, a few hundred miles nearer my destination of Tashkent. I felt a sense of excitement as I boarded the train. But every seat was taken. I stumbled over boxes and bags, the personal possessions of the evacuees who were fleeing Moscow hoping to find safety in the south. I stood in the corridor until a young boy got up and offered me his seat. I took it, grateful to be out of the limelight since I still felt conspicuous in my new uniform. Digging into my coat pocket, I pulled out a rouble and handed it to the boy who immediately stuffed it into his pocket, grinning broadly. I covertly observed my travelling companions. They were a mixed bunch of workers, evacuees, militia and NKVD. The train got up a good speed, missing out the smaller stations.

I closed my eyes and tried to meditate, blocking out the events of the past few days in order to start thinking about my cover story. I told myself to keep calm, to use my intelligence, to think carefully what my response would be if I were challenged. I owed it to Dimitriev and Irena not to endanger their lives. I had to survive. These thoughts spun round in my head as I slowly let a feeling of calm spread through my body.

We'd been travelling for over half an hour before the railway inspector entered the carriage. He began to check the tickets, most of them held by the evacuees, and the railway passes of the workers. I had my story ready and whispered a silent prayer that he'd find no loopholes. As he approached me, I opened a new packet of tobacco and casually asked him if he'd like a cigarette, one railwayman to another. Cigarettes were a great luxury for everyone during the war. As he reached for the tobacco, I noticed his nicotine-stained fingers and yellowing teeth. I'd made the right decision! I gave him a light and he inhaled deeply. After a moment or two, he asked me my name and where I came from. I launched into my story.

'My name is Yuri. I've been to see my mother and dad in Perm. My dad's been very ill but I hope now that spring's almost here, he'll make some improvement. I'm off back now to my depot in Tashkent. Actually, the journey up here opened my eyes about the war. I keep hearing there's a shortage of recruits for the army so when I get back I think I'll probably join up.'

He nodded in agreement. He told me his name was Nicolai, working on the lines between Perm and Aralsk. He was too old to join the army and rather unfit, he said, exaggerating his cough and tapping his chest. He inhaled again and I relaxed. As a railway employee, I was allowed free travel and he didn't need to see my pass, my uniform was enough. We chatted until he'd finished his cigarette. He got up to go, saying he'd got work to do. The trains were so busy with all the evacuees. I told him to come back for another cigarette when he'd got a moment.

When he'd gone I could relax properly. My neck muscles ached, the seats were uncomfortable and although I'd been lucky in my first encounter with officialdom, I could feel the tension building up in my head. The regular movement of the train helped to calm me and I found myself repeating over and over again, in time with the tick, tack, tack, tick, tack, tack rhythm of the wheels on the track, Yuri Dimitrievich Petrovsky, Yuri Dimitrievich Petrovsky. The movement and noise was hypnotic and I eventually fell into a deep sleep. In my dreams, I remembered the lessons drilled into me at the Jesuit college: 'Silence is golden, speak only when spoken to.'

Waking up, I realised the importance of these words. I had a slight accent and whilst ordinary civilians mightn't notice, NKVD officers would be likely to note the difference.

The train had emptied slightly and there were a few vacant seats. Moving to a more comfortable position by the window, I could relax against the side of the carriage. Nicolai was checking tickets again. I hastily lit a cigarette, keeping the packet on my knee ready to offer him tobacco. He was followed by a stunning young woman.

'Ah, Yuri, maybe you're in need of some female company on your long journey?'

He introduced me. The young woman's name was Lydia and she was also travelling to Tashkent. As he spoke he was already rolling his cigarette.

'Lydia was sharing a carriage with common evacuees and dirty peasants. I told her you're a friend of mine and would be good company for her.'

As we said hello, I felt apprehensive since she looked at me with an air of authority and I was terse in reply to her first questions. In another situation I would have welcomed her company since she was quite beautiful. Her raven-black hair was plaited and tied round her head to form a crown. Deep-set, brown eyes dominated her features. She was well-dressed, wearing knee-length brown boots and a thick fur coat pulled tightly across her body. My mind slipped back to the Lubianka, remembering Natasha in her high-heeled boots, and I involuntarily shuddered.

'Are you cold?' she asked.

'No, I've been asleep. It's a long tedious journey.'

Obviously starved of conversation in her previous compartment, she proceeded to tell me about herself. She was a student at Moscow University, the daughter of a colonel in the Soviet army. As the Germans moved closer to the city, her father had ordered her to go to stay with friends in Tashkent who were quite willing to put her up until the crisis was over. As she continued to bore me with her flippant conversation, I noticed how she fidgeted in her seat. My curiosity finally got the better of me and I asked why she didn't sit still.

'It's the lice. I must have picked them up in that filthy carriage.'

Jokingly, I said she couldn't have caught them from me but even as I spoke I began to feel itchy. Lice spread like wildfire when people were cramped together. I knew this only too well from my experience of that horrific journey to Pechora Camp.

I remained quiet not wanting to be drawn into conversation about myself, but she didn't seem to mind my silence and was quite happy to do the talking. She began to make comments about recent events and it soon became clear that her father had taught her well. She said, for example, that the powerful Soviet army was retreating not because the Germans were stronger but because the Russians were more intelligent and didn't want to take too many casualties in bloody battles. It would be a different matter when the Germans reached the Urals because the Russian generals would then put their plans into operation. They would surround the German forces and finish them off!

I smiled to myself, thinking this was rather typical Stalinist propaganda. She continued in the same vein. Winston Churchill, understanding the danger from Hitler, had signed an alliance with Russia which, according to Lydia, was the greatest success yet for Soviet foreign policy, the result of putting into practice Lenin's doctrine of how 'to take advantage of the conflicts existing between the imperialist states'. As she warmed up, the party line came over loud and clear.

'The Soviet Union is a freedom-loving nation and carries a heavy burden in the struggle against Fascists and Imperialists. Victory in the struggle for freedom for the entire world rests on the shoulders of the Soviet people and especially on the Russian army under the supreme command of our beloved hero, Stalin.'

I began to curse Nicolai for introducing me to this woman. But she wasn't finished yet.

'England is a powerful country although they are Capitalists and Imperialists. We, the students of Moscow, believe that soon England will be ruled by Russia, thus freeing them from the oppressions of Capitalism. We are the pioneers who introduced Communism and the complete freedom of all our people!'

So great was her exuberance that she became flushed with excitement as she continued to lecture me on the merits of freedom. My mind flashed back to my days in Siberia where I'd been envious of the rats, where a horse was classed as more important than a human being, where millions of men, women and children were starving and others were being tortured while

129

their friends died from hunger and overwork. I wanted to tell her this was the true story of Stalin's regime, this was their so-called freedom!

At the same time I felt sorry for this young, attractive student who had been indoctrinated so young. But I had to keep quiet; any word against Communism would seal my fate. I wanted my own brand of freedom, and her and my definitions of that word were totally at odds. I'd learned enough to know that her attempts to engage me in her political discussions were just a trap.

Failing to draw me out, she allowed me a few moments of silence whilst she studied her hands, but she couldn't keep quiet for long. She now began to delve into my personal life, asking me about my family, my work, my home. The questions were endless. I told her what I'd told Nicolai, stressing my intention to join the army on my return to Tashkent. Night fell.

'I'm tired and these seats are so uncomfortable. May I rest my head on your knee?'

I moved, settling myself into the corner. She moved closer to me, her warm body against mine. Resting her head on my knee she soon fell asleep. I was not long behind. We were both hypnotised by the tick, tack, tack of the train. Suddenly we were jolted back to life by the screech of the brakes. We were approaching Chelyabinsk.

Out of the steamed-up windows I could see smart houses and factories, with smoke pouring out of their chimneys. This was in stark contrast to the desolate lands of Siberia. Chelyabinsk was the largest city in Bashkir province. We moved steadily into the station. The buildings were massive and on the four or five platforms were crowds of people. We were both hungry. Many people were boarding the train and Lydia offered to keep our seats while I went in search of food. Chelyabinsk was a carbon copy of Kotlas and Perm. Soldiers queued for hot water, NKVD and railway officials queued for food and hot tea, and civilians queued for provisions. The militia kept a strict eye on the queues, walking up and down continuously.

I joined the queue for the cafeteria, at the same time keeping alert to the movements of the NKVD officers and the militia. Their constant patrolling began to make me feel nervous but I knew that they were on the look-out for signs of nerves and so I affected boredom, nonchalantly lighting a cigarette and blowing the smoke into the air. When it was my turn to be served, I hurriedly asked the assistant for two cups of tea and some cheesecake, adding that one tea was for my travelling companion, a student at Moscow University. 'Moscow' was a magic word: two large pieces of cheesecake and two hot teas were handed to me. I paid my money, smiling cheekily at the NKVD officer nearby.

The train was now crammed with passengers. Hundreds of Kazakhs had boarded the train. The majority of them were filthy, their clothes ragged. They smelt of stale sweat and their hands were forever scratching their bodies, disturbing the hungry lice. The majority of them were barefoot and each carried a rough sack of provisions with him. I couldn't help overhearing their conversation. They were recent recruits for the Soviet army, travelling to Orsk for initial military training. These semi-literate youths had obviously been promised great rewards for their commitment to the Russian cause. Their conversation was raucous, their language vulgar and offensive. They had obviously grown up in an environment where profanities were the norm. Lydia tried to ignore the filthy language. Since the influx of these Kazakhs she just made polite conversation and dropped her close questioning of me.

Soon their conversation turned to Lydia. They discussed her body and her hair. One man getting terribly excited, began to describe in detail what he would like to do to her. She became flushed with embarrassment. I told her to ignore them. But the offensive banter continued and I thought I heard a hint of fear in her voice as she asked me to step in, in my official capacity, to moderate their language. I explained that, since it wasn't my train, I couldn't show my authority but I said I'd fetch Nicolai. I found him in the next carriage and he followed me back. Lydia was becoming hysterical and she turned on Nicolai.

'If this repulsive, despicable language continues any longer I'll have no option but to hold you responsible!'

Sensing trouble, I blended into the background. Nicolai tried to calm the situation but emotions were running high and the Kazakhs ridiculed him. Lydia was enraged. She took out her Communist Party identity pass and in a high-pitched voice asked for Nicolai's work pass number which she noted in her private book 'for further reference'. Then she stood on the wooden seat and shouted at the top of her voice.

'As a member of the Communist Party and a citizen of the Soviet Union, I have the authority to ensure that proper behaviour is observed in public places, especially on the railway, the main form of transport in our beloved country! There are other travellers on this train and they do not wish to listen to your filthy language and your insinuations!'

One of the Kazakhs turned on her, clenching his hand and shaking his fist in the air.

'Who do you think you are, you filthy bitch! Without your fancy clothes you're no better than the rest of us!'

He spat at her, missing her by inches. Realising he'd missed, he lunged forward as if to strike her. Nicolai intervened, preventing the blow reaching its target.

'That's enough! Your pass please! I'll not put up with trouble-makers on my train. There are plenty of NKVD men around, maybe you'd like to strike one of them!'

The ill-feeling subsided. The Kazakh handed Nicolai his pass, somewhat subdued. Nicolai then began to grovel to Lydia, promising to find her better accommodation in the first class carriage which was, of course, reserved for higher officials but he was sure he could explain the situation.

Lydia turned to me, a happy glint in her eyes, and invited me to join her in first class. I was quick to decline, explaining that Nicolai would need my help to control the Kazakhs.

I sat down, relieved that she'd gone. Tashkent was a long way off and the thought of spending the entire journey with her had filled me with dismay. Lost in my thoughts, I was startled when the carriage door was thrown open. Three uniformed militia men entered and arrested the offending Kazakh, dragging him out of the compartment.

I felt sorry for him; he was a spirited youth and it was a pity that his spirit would soon be beaten out of him. The bad language started again, but this time in hushed voices. My heart went out to these young men. From early childhood they'd been brought up like animals, with very little schooling, no social life, and no access to religion. They were simply the property of the Soviet state and now they were old enough, they were ordered to serve it like slaves.

## Chapter Eighteen

# *On to Tashkent*

The incident between the Kazakhs and Lydia, the Moscow student, not surprisingly, unnerved me. I knew how important it was for me to stay out of trouble, not only for my own safety, but also to protect Dimitriev and Irena. That incident showed me how vulnerable I was. I couldn't afford to become involved in such incidents if I was to keep a low profile. To be sure, I felt more secure now that Lydia was safely in another compartment, and I was certainly relieved to be free of her probing questions.

Outside, the landscape had changed. The booming industry and smart houses of Chelyabinsk had been left behind and we were now travelling through a vast agricultural area, where fields of tall yellow grass were interrupted by gently rolling green hills crossed by narrow farmroads. This was the Kirghiz steppe. From the carriage window it presented a picture of peace and tranquility but when I looked more closely I saw that there were very few inhabited farm houses. Moreover, the beauty of the scene was marred by the desolate wooden barracks roughly erected in the fields at regular intervals. In fact most of the fields had gone back to nature, and weeds were more evident than sown crops.

I sat staring out of the window, appalled at this waste of good agricultural land. My thoughts were uninterrupted since even the Kazakhs were quiet, no doubt drained and tired by the excitement of the last few hours. I smiled to myself as they puffed avidly on their rolled cigarettes. After the rumpus over Lydia, one of them had asked, rather bravely in the circumstances, if I would swap some of my tobacco for a piece of cheese. This sparked off other requests. I was surprised that they'd offer me the earth for just one cigarette. This bartering kept me in bread and cheese for the rest of the journey. On arrival at Orsk, the Kazakhs got out. There they were quickly formed into columns and marched away under the stern eye of a Soviet army corporal. As I watched them out of sight. I wondered how many of them would survive the war and return to their homes.

I'd been told by Nicolai that the train would stop in Orsk for an hour, so I decided to stretch my legs and go to the station cafeteria for a warm drink. The station here was a hive of activity with hundreds of newly-trained soldiers swarming all over the plat-forms. They looked smart in their brand-new uniforms, these peasant boys, but now they were off to the front for their first taste of active service. Their rifles were slung across their shoulders and ammunition belts hung round their waists but I was astonished to see that none of them had any ammunition. I learned later that the basic training was so intensive that some of the recruits became unbalanced and attacked their officers and anyone near them. Hence ammunition was not distributed until they reached the battle area.

I waited in the 'Officials Only' queue. The NKVD and the militia were, as usual, on patrol. I was used to them giving me the 'once over' and no doubt speculating why I wasn't in the army. But my uniform still protected me and I was never actually questioned. The hot tea, though weak, was wonderfully refreshing and the cheesecake, which was only available to officials, was definitely filling. I felt well prepared for the next stage of the journey.

Returning to my compartment, I settled myself into the corner seat. Most of the passengers were newly-trained soldiers travelling to Kandagach where they would get a connection to Guryev, one stage nearer the front. In appearance they were not as rough as the Kazakhs. Fresh out of training they were ready for anything, or so they thought. I smiled to myself as I listened to their conversations about the 'German pigs' and how they alone would rid their mother country of these bastards. I particularly noticed that their uniforms were made from fine-quality material, far superior to those of the NKVD officials in the camps. I wondered if the material had been sent from Britain as a result of the recent Anglo–Soviet Pact. But enough of this speculation about the outside world! I had my own problems and plans had to be made.

Nicolai was leaving the train at Aralsk and maybe his replacement would not be as pliable, so I had to be sure that my story sounded as convincing to him as it had to Nicolai, otherwise all my efforts would have been wasted. It was midnight when the train drew up in Kandagach. As the soldiers began to file out of the carriage, I decided to risk leaving the train for another hot drink. Although the climate was warmer, the nights were still cold and I stamped my feet to revive the circulation. Hurriedly stepping over sleeping soldiers who were also waiting for the connection for Guryev, I discovered that the café was closed, though boiling water was available. I filled my cup and warmed my hands on it as I made my way back to the train. To my surprise, the compartment was now full and my window seat had been taken. I had great difficulty getting a seat at all. The new passengers were mainly officers on their way to Tashkent to pick up new recruits for training. While we waited for the train to start, they animatedly discussed new training methods.

I suddenly had a feeling that someone was watching me and my eyes were drawn to one of the lieutenants whose face seemed familiar. Where had I seen him before? Thinking furiously I realised, to my horror, that he was the same lieutenant who had ordered me to be shot at Perm. Or was he? I couldn't be absolutely sure. So it was an enormous relief when Nicolai came into the compartment. The extra warmth of my greeting was designed to divert the officer's attention and to remove any possible suspicions. When I complained about the over-crowding in the compartment, Nicolai offered to find me somewhere quieter, apparently sensing my discomfort at the presence of all these officers. I tried to relax but I was doing everything wrong. Showing signs of unease was a sure way of getting myself arrested.

I closed my eyes and took a deep breath but could not shake off the feeling that I was being watched. From my new seat I could still see the lieutenant, who was now talking to a civilian at the far end of the carriage. I felt sure this was just a ruse and all the time he was observing me. I felt trapped, wanting to get up and run but knowing this would be fatal. I had to act perfectly naturally if I wanted to avoid arrest.

Standing up, I made my way to the toilet, debating whether to risk waiting for the train to stop or to take the bull by the horns and jump to safety. As I agonised over what to do my mind was made up for me by the train coming to a stop at a place called Chelkar. It was very early morning and as usual the station was heavily congested. Pushing my way through crowds of soldiers, I joined the queue at the café, all the time keeping a close watch on the door. I was beginning to get paranoid. My imagination and my overactive mind were playing games with me. I tried to convince myself that the lieutenant couldn't possibly recognise me. Could he?

Suddenly I saw him standing outside the café with the civilian and an NKVD officer. I surmised that the civilian was a high-ranking officer in the militia. I began to panic. Slowly I edged my way to the side door, trying not to look too conspicuous. The three of them were engaged in a lively conversation, not actually looking inside the café. I slipped through the door and found myself in a small enclosed yard littered with rubbish. The wall was about four feet high and I jumped it easily enough. I headed surreptitiously back to the platform, watching the train while keeping a lookout for the lieutenant and his companions. When the train at last began to move, I waited until the last passenger carriage reached the end of the platform before jumping aboard. Looking back at the now distant station, I was sure I saw the lieutenant and his friends pushing their way through the throngs of soldiers. My relief that they had missed the train was overwhelming.

I could now take notice of my immediate surroundings. I had ended up in a filthy, rubbish-strewn, third-class carriage. The passengers were mostly dirty and uncouth peasants who eyed me with suspicion, though my uniform earned respect and they did not query my presence. It was naturally a surprise to Nicolai to find me in this glorified cattle truck. This was to be the last of our meetings since by the late afternoon we would arrive in Aralsk, where he ended his tour of duty. He was excited at the prospect of two days' leave with his wife and family before making the monotonous return journey to Perm.

As soon as we reached Aralsk I headed for the café since I didn't want to face a new inspector without food and drink inside me. Huge signs hung in every window: NO CIVILIANS ALLOWED WITHOUT AUTHORITY and THIS CAFETERIA IS FOR OFFICIAL USE ONLY. I hesitated momentarily but I was in uniform, I was an official and, most of all, I was hungry. Taking a deep breath I opened the door. The café was not very busy. I ordered a cup of tea, bread and a boiled egg! What luxury! Taking the feast to an empty table, I began to savour every mouthful. Unfortunately my privacy was soon invaded. Heading towards my table was a well-dressed man carrying a suitcase and balancing his tea precariously in his left hand. Following him, and obviously his companion, was an NKVD officer.

I felt uncomfortable and hoped it didn't show. They began to make polite conversation.

Opening his suitcase the man took out a bottle of vodka and put it on the table. A packet of English cigarettes followed. When he offered me one I declined, producing my packet of *machorka* instead.

'This tobacco is stronger. Have one of mine.'

Both men took some tobacco and began to roll their cigarettes.

'Real luxury,' the man said. 'I haven't had such strong tobacco in months! Finish your tea and help us drink this vodka.'

He filled my cup three-quarters full and I downed it in one. Kissing the cup and raising it in the air, a Russian custom, I toasted Stalin. Then I made the excuse of a train to catch and left as quickly as I could. In my new second class compartment the vodka began to make me feel light-headed. Before long the replacement inspector appeared, accompanied by a militia man. He was inspecting all tickets and passes. I hoped my uniform would be my pass. When they approached I blew a cloud of smoke in the air and offered them tobacco. I was relieved when they accepted. Light conversation followed and Nicolai's name was mentioned. I spoke of our friendship and of my intention of joining the army on my return to Tashkent. The inspector pulled a face. He'd only leave the railway when he received his call-up papers. I said it wouldn't be too long before we all received them: meanwhile I thought we had a duty to defend our Motherland.

The militia man shrugged and walked off but the inspector lingered, obviously savouring his cigarette.

'I think you might be more comfortable in a third class compartment,' he said. 'Most of the first and second class seats have been reserved for senior army officers at the next station. You might feel a bit uncomfortable surrounded by them!'

He seemed to watch closely my reaction to this news. It was obvious that Nicolai had been discussing me. I gave him enough tobacco for another cigarette and thanked him for the offer of a different seat. I'd had enough of the company of military types on this trip, I told him, and was hoping to get some sleep. A quiet corner would be appreciated. I was soon installed in my new seat with the time to reflect and to consider my next step. One thing was clear: my *machorka* was running out and I'd have to go easy on giving it away on the train. I decided to keep the last packet for bribes since I wasn't sure I could replace it in Tashkent.

I soon discovered that the inspector's warning about the military was correct. As the train pulled into the station, I could see generals, top officials of the NKVD, plus all their plain-clothes advisers and hundreds of soldiers. The generals and officials promptly took over the first and second class compartments while the soldiers waited on the platform for more carriages to be added. The train was now so long that a second locomotive had to be coupled up to push from behind. I watched the soldiers as they waited. Their hair was cropped very short and their uniforms showed the signs of battle. These were not new recruits; they'd just come back from the front. They looked like lambs who'd defied slaughter, hungry, frightened and demoralised, as they waited for the order to board the train. Each one gave the impression of wishing he'd never volunteered for this terrible conflict.

I thought of my own life in the Polish army. Although conditions had been strict, there was really no comparison between them and what these Russian soldiers were having to endure. I found it impossible to believe that these soldiers were physically and mentally fit enough to fight the Germans. My heart went out to them, yet I wanted the Russians to be defeated, not because defeat would cause them misery but because it would free Russia from the slavery of Communism and the labour camps. At least, I reflected, I had tasted freedom in my native Poland; these young men had never known it. When the train stopped at Novokazalinsk, the generals, officials and troops departed, lining up on the platform for transport to their next rendezvous as military backup for the newly-formed Kazakhstan Army.

With the aid of my helpful inspector, I could now resume my seat in second class and the regular motion of the train soon sent me to sleep. I awoke to beautiful sunshine as the train ran down the valley of the Syr-Darya which flows into the Aral Sea. While I slept, new passengers had come into my compartment and I now found myself in the company of several Uzbekh and Kirghiz peasants. They were dressed in rags. Their skins were weatherbeaten and pock-marked from the effects of smallpox. Life should have been paradise for them in this beautiful valley with its miles and miles of fertile soil and a climate warmer than the Rhineland. But the paradise was empty. Stalin's collective and state farms had transformed this lush farmland into a barren waste. Peasant resistance to collectivisation had been crushed by mass deportations to the labour camps. The 'lucky conformists' were allowed bread and a makeshift bed in the communal barracks, where between four and eight families shared a room, their only privacy supplied by sacking strung across the room to form tiny compartments. Their greatest indignity, perhaps, was being compelled to praise the Soviet system as 'heaven on earth' and to mouth the then fashionable slogan 'It is good to work on the communal farms'.

I saw the misery etched on the faces of these peasants and I realised the sharp contrast between their lives and those of the NKVD officials and army officers whose neat houses and compact gardens we were now passing. These were in the suburbs of Tashkent. I had reached the end of the line. As the train pulled into the station I felt vulnerable, since this train had been my home for many days. As I stepped onto the platform, I felt as if I was becoming independent for the first time.

# Chapter Nineteen

## *Tashkent: Black Market, Soviet Style*

Wandering the cobbled streets of the ancient city of Tashkent, I couldn't help being amused that war and twenty years of Communism had not persuaded the Muslim traders to join the cooperatives. Black markets seemed to flourish in this city.

It soon became apparent that anything could be bought at a price. There was lots of bread, eggs, fruit and vegetables in the bustling market place, along with hardware goods which were usually in very short supply in the Soviet Union. Here, provided you had the money, you could buy anything without even having to show your government work certificate. Since I had the money, my priority was to fill my empty stomach.

The traders were surprised to see a uniformed man looking over their goods since most officials bought from the huge cooperatives, where food was about one third of the price in the markets. The mouth-watering smell of fresh baking bread drew me to a bread stall. When I asked for three loaves, the middle-aged woman behind the stall held out her hand for the money in advance. Placing three roubles in the palm of her hand, I watched the look of delight spread across her face. This was not surprising, since the average wage for a Russian worker at that time was about four roubles a week.

Large baskets of boiled eggs were on display at the adjacent stall. I hurriedly bought twelve, tempted to purchase the entire basket. I was so absorbed in my quest for food that I was quite oblivious of the presence of two Arabs who were watching my movements very closely as I was to discover later. Desperately hungry, I hurriedly found an empty bench away from the general bustle of the market, tore into the loaf and shelled the eggs, managing to eat about six before my throat cried out for mercy.

It was only now, in this quiet corner, that I sensed I was being watched. I looked around but could see no one. Since I was now very thirsty, I made for the crowded market place where I would, in any case, be safer. I found a market café. As I entered, all eyes turned towards me. I knew immediately I'd made a mistake since railway personnel invariably used the railway cafés. I began to feel rather conspicuous in my uniform. Though the coffee was hot and sweet, the first cup did nothing to cease the clogged feeling in the back of my throat. I ordered a second cup. Generously tipping the assistant I asked him where I could buy the best vodka in the market place. He didn't answer but hurried away to his safe haven behind the counter. He was soon engaged in a whispered conversation by two Arabs who had come into the café as I was ordering my first cup of coffee.

I began to feel uneasy. Were these men following me? Had I fallen into a trap? Was I in the power of informers? Though my hunger was satisfied, I could feel the panic rising deep in the pit of my stomach. The three men were obviously talking about me to judge from their furtive glances in my direction. A fourth man, another Arab, who seemed to be the café proprietor, joined them. I fought the panic, having already bluffed my way out of numerous dangerous situations. Was there any reason why I should fail this time? Suddenly I saw the proprietor walking towards me, a solemn, worried look on his face.

'You were asking my assistant about vodka. Why don't you buy it from the cooperative? With your work card you must be able to get a discount.'

I was about to make an excuse when an NKVD man walked into the café. My heart sank. I was sure now that the Arabs were informers and that my cover was blown and that any moment I'd be arrested. The proprietor seemed aware of my nervousness, but then surprised me by saying, with a glance at the NKVD man: 'He's one of us but if he makes you nervous, follow me.'

He took me to a tiny room next to the kitchens. Opening a small cabinet he handed me a glass and produced a bottle of fine Russian vodka. I took a drink, letting the hot liquid burn my throat. He watched me as I drained my glass.

'Now then, my friend, shall we talk? Don't worry, you're quite safe here, but we know what you've been doing in Tashkent. You surely must have been aware of my colleagues tailing you and watching you buy food. Your behaviour easily gives you away. You're not like ordinary Russians; your accent's sharper and you throw money around. I guess there's something you'd like to tell me. Don't worry, I'm not an official or an informer and if you're in trouble I may be able to help you. But if you've come to spy on me and my friends for the authorities you're as good as dead. So, let's have the truth. I want to know why you're here.'

I needed time to think. Why was this man offering to help a perfect stranger? Had I stumbled into the arms of a counter-revolutionary organisation? I did the only thing possible, which was to play for time. I told him I wasn't what I appeared to be and he could rely on me as a friend. But I needed help.

'If you're telling the truth I can help you, though I'm only an intermediary. I can give you the address of a house here in Tashkent where they will help you but I must warn you again – if you're not genuine you'll not leave that house alive. To get admission you'll need this!'

Opening a small box, he handed me a round white cardboard disc the size of a coin. I looked puzzled. He explained that 'all our people' carried one of these 'pass cards'. If I was arrested I should swallow it since it contained cyanide and death would be instantaneous. They didn't want 'their friends' to face gruelling interrogations and to place 'their organisation' in jeopardy.

I thanked him for his help though still unsure about his intentions. Perhaps I was getting too involved with these people and endangering my chances of escape. Yet I was curious, and as I left the café I felt fairly certain I'd eventually go to the address that had been hastily scribbled on a small piece of scrap paper. Meanwhile I wandered the streets buying tea and sugar cubes for later on and small items such as saccharines which I'd not seen in years. Now I had more time to look about me I noticed how many different ethnic groups were represented in the crowded market place and how the NKVD and the militia seemed to turn a blind eye to the bartering and selling going on around them.

The two Arabs were still following me and I began to wonder whether they were more concerned for my safety or for the safety of their precious disc. But wandering round the streets cleared my mind and I reached a decision. Leaving the market by a side alley, I went in search of the address I'd been given, feeling confident that I was doing the right thing.

The building wasn't hard to find. I got no reply to my first knock on the heavy door. Knocking again, I heard the sound of keys turning in a lock. As the door opened, I saw a tall, thick-set Arab towering above me, filling the doorway with his presence. He totally ignored me even when I mentioned the café owner. In desperation I slowly opened my hand to show him the disc in my palm. Immediately his attitude changed. Bowing, he stood aside and beckoned me to enter. I was aware of the key turning in the lock behind me as my eyes adjusted to the dim light.

I was ushered through a bamboo curtain into a spacious room where four more Arabs were seated at the table. They stood up as I entered, their eyes examining my uniform. Immediately the questioning started. They were sharp and ruthless. I stuck to my original story, telling them that my duties were to supervise the railway line between Perm and Moscow. 'Why are you in Tashkent? Why have you been given this address? Where did you obtain so much money?'

I hesitated, not wanting to incriminate my friends. One of the Arabs was quick to spot my hesitation and standing over me demanded the truth. Since I was obviously not Russian – my accent was too harsh – maybe I would feel more at ease speaking in my own tongue? I looked at each man in turn. Should I take the

145

risk of telling them the truth? They seemed to have power, perhaps they could help me to escape. I decided to gamble everything on the truth. In my best Russian I told them my story. They listened intently, never once interrupting me. As I neared the end of my tale, they began to smile.

'You are a very brave man. You don't know how close you were to losing your life. We're very wary of government officials; in the past we've murdered them for their uniforms alone. Naturally, if we're going to protect our own people, we have to dispose of any official who stumbles on our organisation.'

I began to relax. My main interrogator pulled out a packet of tobacco and offered me genuine cigarette papers. One of his colleagues took up the conversation.

'We're a big organisation dealing in smuggled goods, which are brought into the country across the Persian and Afghan borders. We have lots of contacts, even many in the NKVD, the militia and the army who betray their country for extra money. These contacts help to transport the contraband to us once it's crossed the border. Naturally we have rules for dealing with informers and they're very simple – we kill them and feed their bodies to the pigs.'

Pausing for breath, he opened a door to show me the Aladdin's cave inside – wines, spirits, tobacco, hams, cheeses, and many other goods which had long since vanished from shop counters. Boxes of these items were stacked as high as the ceiling. He boasted that you could buy anything from them and if they hadn't got it in stock they'd arrange for a delivery. At this, he opened a bottle of vodka to prove his hospitality though he said he didn't drink alcohol as a rule. Filling five glasses, he handed one to each of his friends and gave me the last one full to the brim. As we drank, he encouraged me to talk about my plans. I told him I hoped to reach the Afghan border.

They immediately began to offer help. They were planning to send eight carriers to the Persian border to pick up supplies, taking sheepskins with them as payment. If I was willing to take twenty-five kilograms of sheepskins on my back I was welcome to join them. 'The leader is an experienced man who has travelled the route to Persia many times.'

It was an attractive proposition but when he told me I would have to leave my uniform and dress as an Arab I hesitated. It was obvious that my uniform was of great importance to them since it would enable them to infiltrate the railway system. They could place one of their men on the trains to supervise the carrying of supplies, thus cutting out the risk of ambush by bandits on the lonely mountain passes. They tried to persuade me.

'It's unwise to travel alone. I've lost twenty of my best men recently. If the bandits don't get them the army patrols arrest them and send them to the camps. Army garrisons are spread right along the Afghan border, so there's a great risk. You'll be safer travelling to Persia.'

I shook my head. I was adamant that I was going to Afghanistan. I knew I couldn't back down. Even though these men were ruthless, they seemed to respect me. I felt quite safe in their company since they knew I was fighting for my freedom. I was confident that they wouldn't demand my uniform, or my life. They continued to be free with their advice, however, and played down my chances of survival on the Afghan border. Once I crossed the Amu Darya river, which was patrolled by the Soviet army, then I would enter no man's land, a hotbed of thieves, smugglers and fugitives who lived in their own little world between the Amu Darya and the Afghan border. Here I could trust no one and my life would constantly be at risk.

I explained that my plans involved using the railway for part of the journey, at least as far as Samarkand. After that I hoped to make my way to Karshi and thence to Kerki and finally across the border. Again I received advice. The Kerki bridge was extremely dangerous and I should only attempt to cross during darkness. Many people were arrested on that bridge and rumour had it that a cattle truck waited permanently in the railway sidings for people apprehended on the crossing. When it was full it conveyed its load of prisoners to the camps.

I thanked them for their warning. Their response was touching.

'We're also fighting for our freedom, that's why we sympathise with you. We'll pray to Allah for your safe-keeping. May He help you to survive your ordeal and win your struggle for freedom.'

We talked for hours. They were very interested in my horrific accounts of life in the camps and how I'd planned my escape. The vodka loosened my tongue and I told them about the severe frosts, the gangrene caused by frostbite, the extreme hunger and deprivation, the red flag being printed with the blood of prisoners, the bodies of the dead and dying being stripped of their clothes and fed to the wolves. How, as well, my own horse had been eaten alive because it would not leave me. Finally I showed them my neck, the scar still red and ugly, as I related the story of the attempt to kill me. They were horrified by my experiences but hopeful that I would make it over the border to freedom.

Despite their offer of a bed for the night, I felt it would be safer if I found an old railway truck near the station. They insisted that I keep the disc as a gift for use if I was caught. Then we parted with an embrace and the blessing of Allah.

Earlier that morning, I'd checked the timetable at the station. The train to Samarkand was due to leave at eight o'clock the following morning. I could have taken a goods train leaving at nine that evening but it didn't seem right for a railway inspector to travel like that. Walking towards the overgrown sidings, I was filled with a new confidence. The vodka had warmed my blood but, more important, I now knew that I was not the only one fighting for freedom. There were perhaps millions more like me. Sadly, many thousands of them would die in their quest, cut down by the sadistic organs of power.

Checking the goods train, I tried to look official while all the time edging deeper into the tangled undergrowth towards an old disused wagon that had been pushed off the line. Though its doors were rusted and would not close properly, it was dry and there was clean straw on the floor. I decided it would provide a makeshift bed for the night.

My head was slightly woozy from too much vodka so I took some fruit and bread from my case, hoping to soak up some of the alcohol. As it grew dark, the temperature fell and I wished I still had my great fur coat. Pulling straw across my body, I tried to retain some heat. I decided to meditate, shutting out the events of the day in order to clear my mind and finalise my plans. The alcohol began to make me sleepy and I dropped off.

Suddenly I became aware of voices. I sat up, listening intently. There was a rustling of grass and a girl's voice. A man was climbing into the truck, a young girl pushing him from behind. They were totally unaware of my presence in the dark. Standing up, he helped her into the wagon. With nimble fingers she began to undo his clothing. Jumping to my feet. I startled them. The young prostitute leapt out of the wagon and ran off into the darkness, still giggling. The man stood rooted to the spot, his trousers half undone. As he saw my uniform, a look of terror spread across his face.

Calmly I walked round him.

'Why are you trespassing on government property? We heard that these trucks were being used for prostitution. Where are your identity papers?'

He stood in front of me, totally lost for words. I continued to question him, knowing that my uniform gave me the upper hand. The poor man began to apologise.

'She's only a prostitute. I only wanted a good time and now she's run off with my money, cleared me out completely.'

I assumed an official tone.

'That's not my fault. I'm within my rights to report you to the NKVD. I could even arrest you and place you in railway custody. But I'll be lenient since you've done no harm and you've been punished enough – no money, no fun. You'd better go home to your wife and family before I change my mind.'

He bowed his head, fulsome in his gratitude, and cautiously backed out of the wagon. I gathered the hay round me and fingered the disc in my pocket to make sure it was still safe. As I closed my eyes. I had to smile as I conjured up the image of the interloper, with his trousers slipping down his thin legs, hoping he was going to get some enjoyment in his drab life, only to be interrupted at the last minute by a man in uniform.

# Chapter Twenty

## *Tashkent to Samarkand*

I awoke to bright sunshine. Dusting the straw from my uniform, I settled down to eat a hearty breakfast. My head ached, the result of too much vodka, but the events of the previous day had worked to my advantage and a slight headache was a small price to pay. Checking my uniform for stray wisps of hay, I made sure the coast was clear before making my way back to the station.

The train hadn't arrived yet and I wandered up and down the platform, stopping to study the maps, trying to keep calm. Suddenly I saw the familiar faces of the two Arabs who'd been tailing me the day before. They were standing some distance away but were still watching me closely.

When the train arrived I was drawn into the mêlée of passengers trying to leave the train at the same time as others were desperately pushing and shoving to get a seat. For a few seconds I felt lost in the turmoil but suddenly the two Arabs were at my side. Gripping my arms, they bludgeoned their way on to the train and took me to a second class compartment where I managed to secure a window seat. When I turned to thank them they'd already disappeared.

My carriage was almost full, most of the passengers being officials of some sort, or army officers. Two army corporals sat down opposite me. They were about my own age and looked rather impressive in their smart uniforms and highly polished boots.

However, when I took out my tobacco and my treasured cigarette papers and began to roll a cigarette they couldn't keep their eyes off my hands. They were quite obviously desperate for a smoke. I took pity on them and offered them enough tobacco for two cigarettes. One of them quickly tore two strips from the front page of his newspaper. Noticing that he'd ripped across a large picture of Stalin I leaned towards him and whispered in his ear. Tearing a picture of our 'beloved Stalin' was just the way to get himself arrested since the train was full of officials and informers just waiting for the chance to report a foolhardy young corporal who forgot to treat his leader with respect.

As a gesture of friendship I gave each of them a cigarette paper. The one with the newspaper blushed as he furtively tucked it back into his pocket. 'Thank you,' he whispered, 'thank you.' They made polite conversation between deep drags on their cigarettes. They'd been trying to buy *machorka* in Tashkent but the prices were too high for them on the black market and the cheap tobacco in their rations only lasted them two days. To allay suspicion, I confided that I'd just received my own tobacco ration but had managed to swap it for *machorka* paying a slight difference in roubles. This story seemed to satisfy them.

After a while I found their conversation rather boring and gazed idly round the compartment. My two Arab minders were sitting by the door of the carriage and nodded in recognition when our eyes met. But I felt others were watching me too. Seated opposite but further down the compartment was a rather distinguished-looking middle-aged man. He was immaculately dressed in a dark grey suit and wore a pair of rimless glasses. His eyes were deep and penetrating and I fought to hold his gaze, not wanting to be the first to look away. Eventually he glanced at another passenger and I felt the uncomfortable feeling disappear. It seemed very clear to me that he was some sort of high official who should definitely not be crossed.

The inspector arrived. He was an older man with greying hair and thick glasses, and didn't seem very approachable. Reaching in my pocket for my pass, I touched the round white disc and felt a sense of security. When he approached I handed him my pass and drew his attention to the hammer and sickle, 'the sign of authority', stamped across it. As one colleague to another I offered him a cigarette, which he refused. He became officious.

'I'm sorry, but you're travelling in a second class compartment. A pass only entitles you to travel third, as you well know.'

I protested. I wasn't the only one travelling in the wrong compartment. Third class was full of people standing shoulder to shoulder. One of the corporals opposite supported me and other passengers muttered their agreement. Offering him an olive branch, I said I'd gladly go with him if he could find me a seat in third.

The inspector looked helplessly around and for one awful moment I thought the distinguished looking official was going to intervene. Happily for me he remained seated. Shrugging his shoulders the inspector turned away to check the tickets of the remaining passengers. One of the corporals laughed.

'You sorted him out! What a miserable bugger! Fancy not accepting a cigarette!'

I felt obliged to defend him; he was only doing his job, after all. But the two corporals were now in high spirits, telling jokes and making light-hearted comments. Half listening, I suddenly became aware of the reappearance of the inspector with a militia man in close attendance. My instinct for danger told me to avoid trouble. Making the excuse of going to the toilet, I slipped out of the compartment and made my way to the third class section. Though it was full, with a little bit of pushing and shoving I managed to perch on the end of a seat. The peasants and factory workers who made up the bulk of the passengers all moved up a little. Anyone in uniform constituted a threat in their eyes; it just wasn't sensible to alienate authority.

I'd been settled for a good half hour when the inspector appeared yet again, this time alone. I showed some irritation this time and asked what was wrong now. His reply was surprising.

'I've come to apologise. I know you're a colleague and I wouldn't normally have said anything, but the man in the corner was watching me and we'd been warned that some top man was going to be on this train. I didn't want to lose my job. Besides, we've had a lot of trouble on this line. Arab smugglers have managed to infiltrate the railway staff and placed some of their men among the inspectors. So we've had our instructions to be very strict and to check every passenger.'

I looked at him in pretended amazement.

'Surely you don't think I'm a smuggler! You've seen my pass!'

'No, no, it's just that I've got to be extremely careful. You know the rules – I could be prosecuted for allowing passengers to stay in the wrong compartments. When I saw you leave I knew you understood and I was grateful. That's why I've come to apologise.'

I accepted his apology and offered him the cigarette which he'd refused earlier. He didn't need asking a second time, gratefully accepting the proffered tobacco. Looking round the compartment, he thought I was better off where I was, since the other passengers would respect my uniform.

We chatted until he'd finished his cigarette. His name was Georgi. He was coming up to retirement and he desperately wanted the war to end quickly. Two of his sons were in the army and his daughter was married to a Frenchman, now living in France, whom he hadn't heard from for many months. We parted the best of friends.

As the train wound its way through the mountains, I eventually managed to get a seat by the window but it was impossible to get comfortable since the seats were old wooden benches without upholstery. After a while my legs ached and my buttocks became numb. Looking through the carriage window to divert myself, I noticed raggedly-dressed, bare-footed Uzbek peasants working on the mountain slopes. Their primitive huts were dotted here and there, most of them close to the line. Their behaviour formed a curious pattern. As the train reached them, they would run alongside, scrambling in the undergrowth for the lumps of bread and the coins which the better-off passengers threw to them out of the train windows. Like seagulls they fought among themselves for the spoils. I felt acutely sorry for these poor people who, before the war, had mostly been independent shepherds, tending their flocks on the rugged mountainsides. Now they were reduced to fighting among themselves in order to survive. I reflected on the fact that when I reached Samarkand I'd be in Uzbek territory and would have to mix with peasants like these, as I made my way to the Afghan border on foot.

The journey seemed endless. I was much relieved when signs of civilisation began to appear as we approached Samarkand, Tamburlaine's capital in the fourteenth century. I remained in my seat whilst the crowds pushed their way out of the compartment. I was in no hurry to leave since I faced a long, tiring journey on foot and an extra few minutes on the train would not make much difference. When the crowds dispersed, I made my way to the station café. As I drank my tea a feeling of exhilaration flowed over me. I was about to begin the last leg of my journey to freedom. When the two Arabs came into the café, they bought their drinks and approached me.

'You've done well. We'll leave you to continue your journey alone. Do you still have the white disc?'

When I produced it they advised me not to be afraid to use it if necessary. When they'd finished they wished me luck and took the train back to Tashkent.

I decided to replenish my stocks. Since my railway bag was too small to hold the extra provisions I needed for my long journey, I decided to look for something bigger. Black market trading flourished in Samarkand but it was not as obvious as in Tashkent and was also on a smaller scale. Wandering around the shops I eventually found a trader who sold everything. His shop was an Aladdin's cave of boots, clothes, baskets and furniture. Looking around for something appropriate I caught sight of an old suitcase and asked if I could exchange it for my inspector's bag. We bargained a little and, for an extra three roubles, I became the new owner not just of the case but of an enamel boiling pan and an enamel cup as well.

I then returned to the station to study the maps for the last time.

At a rough estimate I had about 200 miles to travel, most of it through the Tadzhikistan mountains. I had a week's supply of food, my hunting knife and my determination. I hoped to travel at least twenty miles a day, drawing confidence from the mild climate, the absence of Siberian wolves and the prospect of travelling through mountains, which had always inspired me in my youth. I was looking forward to seeing the lush greenery again and to smelling the fresh mountain air. I'd made careful plans for the journey. My first stop would be Karshi, about eighty miles away, where I could replenish my stock of food. From there I should make for Kerki, following the course of the railway line south since the mountains were very wild in that area and without a guide I'd almost certainly get lost.

By far the most dangerous part of my journey would be the crossing of the Amu-Darya river. I knew the risks I was taking but my escape had been one long risk. I now had my goal in sight, I had youth on my side, I felt in control and my reward would be my freedom. 'Freedom.' The word sent tingles down my spine. I was physically and mentally ready for this most important part of my journey. If, in the end, I failed, I still had my little white disc and I knew I'd never suffer again at the hands of the sadistic secret police of Joseph Stalin.

# Chapter Twenty-One

## *The Road to Karshi*

The station map was firmly imprinted on my mind. I had to keep heading south but not on the main road since a curfew was in force and any person out after dark was automatically arrested. It was now dusk; all the paths looked alike and, as my Arab friend in Tashkent had warned me, were regularly used by smugglers and thieves. Yet I felt safer wandering through this mountainous terrain than dodging the patrols on the main road.

The mountains loomed up ahead of me. I stood still for a moment looking at their outline in the fading light. Then, with a deep breath, I began my journey. The path was marked by huge stones. The wet grass was slippery and the trees began to blot out what remained of the evening light. My eyes began to adjust to the darkness. I took my time, avoiding risk. Occasionally I would make out the dark silhouette of a tent which I kept well away from, not knowing what to expect from its inhabitants.

Eventually no more tents appeared. I was climbing higher, the night was warm and I breathed the fresh mountain air and thought about my freedom. I walked and walked, spurred on by my thoughts. Then I became aware of a new smell of burning wood. I stopped in the hope of tracing the source of the smell, which I eventually located in a small clearing just off the track. The embers were still glowing and I hurriedly collected small pieces of wood to rekindle the fire. Whoever had lit the fire was also travelling through the night and could only be a little way ahead of me. Since I didn't want any contact with strangers, I decided to rest for a couple of hours.

As the flames began to take hold I hastily collected some stones which I stacked round the base of the fire to contain it. Going in search of water I quickly found a hillside stream nearby where I filled my battered pan. Soon I was drinking hot strong tea. The fresh air had made me ravenously hungry as well. I hurriedly tore my bread into pieces though I rationed myself to two eggs. Propping my case up against a tree, I shut my eyes and pretended that I was on my summer vacation in Zakopane in the Tatras, my family and friends nearby. The smell of the pine trees, the sound of water trickling down, the shape of the valley all reminded me of home. I had to remind myself that this was still the Soviet Union and I was not on summer vacation, that, in fact, I was still on the run. In front of me stretched miles of wild mountainous country. I prayed, finding solace in speaking to God in this peaceful environment, and begged for his guidance in this, the last part of my journey.

I woke with a start. I'd only slept for a couple of hours but it seemed longer. After washing my face with the remaining water, I put out the fire and removed all evidence of my presence. The moon disappeared behind the clouds and it became darker than ever. Setting off again I had to pick my way round pot-holes and was in constant fear of stumbling and breaking my leg.

The darkness produced an eeriness too. Once I was aware of lights flashing in the distance and stopped to watch the circles of light moving up and down, which reminded me of small vessels bobbing on a choppy sea. I couldn't make up my mind whether they were on my path or not. Only when they began to disappear towards the east did it dawn on me that they were the lights of the army patrols on the main road.

At daybreak the air was filled with the strange cries of mountain birds as they began their early morning search for food. I sat down to rest knowing that soon I'd have to find somewhere to sleep. Taking out my precious vodka, I took a large swig to put energy into my tiring body. I found that the higher I climbed the harder it was to stay on the right track. The path was criss-crossed by deep gorges; the only way over was by narrow wooden planks crudely nailed together by previous travellers. In the semi-darkness there was no way of knowing if they were safe. I decided to risk it since I had no time to turn back and look for another route.

As it became lighter I could make out my surroundings more clearly. I decided to climb higher knowing that from the top I would have a good vantage point. When I reached the highest point I was not disappointed. The scenery was breathtaking. A carpet of greenery spread out below me. Mountain streams broke up the tree cover on the slopes like creases on a well-worn photograph. I could see my path beginning to dip down into the valley but parts of it were obscured from view as it twisted through the rows of tall fir trees. I knew that in different circumstances I could have stayed there for ever. The mountains were in my blood.

Suddenly my eyes glimpsed a slight movement two or three miles down the track. I could make out eight or nine people passing through a small clearing, each with a heavy rucksack on his back, probably smugglers, or perhaps bandits. Whoever they were, I had no intention of catching them up. It seemed the right moment to find somewhere to sleep since I suddenly felt exhausted; my eyes were heavy and my legs ached with tiredness. Setting off downhill I wandered off the path to find a secluded spot where I could rest. I soon found one, behind some rocks. A fire and some water from a stream were the only preparations I needed to make a hearty breakfast. I was in heaven. Above me the snow-capped mountain tops, below the lush green of a fertile land. The sun warmed my body and my hunger was satisfied. What more could a man ask for, apart, of course, from the little matter of freedom?

The early sun had, by now, soaked up the morning dew and the grass was dry enough to sleep on. Using my case as a pillow, I lay down in the shelter of the rocks. Sleep came immediately, the previous night's climb having taken most of my energy. I was aware of the warmth of the sun as I changed positions. I slept right through the day and did not wake until the sun began to go down in the early evening.

I felt fresh and alive as I washed in the cool mountain stream and gathered wood to rekindle my fire. While I waited for my water to boil, I found a stout branch and whittled one end into a rough point, thinking that a walking stick might come in useful on my downhill trek. Soon it was to time to set off again. Checking the contents of my case, I found I still had plenty of eggs and bread, a bottle of vodka and three full packets of *machorka*. These were the essentials. I also had tea, sugar and various small items which I hoped would come in useful on the rest of my journey.

The path was steep and stony and other smaller paths joined it as I weaved my way through the trees. At each intersection I would stop, listening for signs of life, not wanting to meet up with anyone, least of all bandits. My alertness paid off. Reaching an intersection I was in complete darkness, the moon being hidden by the trees. Suddenly I became aware of a horse neighing nearby and I dived for the undergrowth. Crouching down in the sweet-smelling grass, I could hear the sound of hooves. Quite quickly men on horseback appeared from the direction of the eastern path. The front rider stopped as if to get his bearings, then with a swift kick he sent his horse charging down the path to Karshi, his patrol following on behind. They appeared to be part of the Kazakh cavalry but I had no idea why they were out in the mountains. I was just thankful that I'd saved myself from arrest.

This incident brought home to me that the mountains had lulled me into a false sense of security. I knew now that I should have to take even more care and keep my wits about me just as I had in Siberia. After a while I resumed my journey, repeating the word 'freedom' over and over again.

After walking non-stop for about five hours, I decided it was time to stop and eat. Reflecting on my journey, with a mug of hot sweet tea in my hand, I was aware in the background of the sounds of nature, the distant howl of a wolf, the bark of a dog in some far-off encampment, the occasional crack of a branch or the rustle of leaves as some wild animal went on its nocturnal search for food. I was not afraid since the wolves fed well in these parts on the numerous sheep who roamed the mountain slopes. I shut my eyes, resting my weary body. If I could just catch an hour's rest I felt I'd be fit to travel for another five hours before finding shelter for the daylight hours.

The sound of a dog barking abruptly ended my doze. I soon realised that it was coming nearer. I quickly spread the dying embers, dusted myself down and gathered my belongings together. Then the barking seemed to stop. Slowly I made my way back to the track, listening intently. I had no idea of the direction from which the barking had come. I walked stealthily, listening for every sound, anything to give me a clue. There was total silence.

Suddenly, from nowhere, the dog appeared, running towards me, teeth bared. My first thought was that it might be rabid. I had only a suitcase and a walking stick with which to defend myself since my hunting knife was locked in the case. I began to swing the case round my body to prevent the dog sinking its teeth into me, all the time hitting out at it with my walking stick. Above the barking and snarling I heard a voice.

'Kill, kill! He's a common bandit!'

A man dressed in a sheepskin jacket and carrying a lantern emerged from the shadows. This Uzbek shepherd, which is what I took him for, stood watching me swinging my case round and round in a desperate attempt to ward off his dog

Suddenly he called the dog to heel and immediately it backed away, baring its teeth and growling softly.

'Thieves and smugglers are the only people out so late at night,' explained the shepherd, somewhat apologetically. 'I have to look after my sheep, you understand. They're always being stolen.'

He shone his lantern up and down.

'You're in uniform. Why are you out in the mountains? You're very lucky, you know. My dog's trained to kill. It was only your suitcase that saved you.'

I embarked on a story about how I'd been to visit my parents and had missed the train back. In a panic I'd decided to walk since it was a three-day wait in Samarkand for the next train and I'd be late for my shift if I didn't reach Karshi on time. Being late for work was a serious offence and I could expect the chop. Soon after I'd set off, though, I'd become totally disorientated and was now desperate to get out of these mountains.

My uniform and my explanation seemed to satisfy him. I invited him to have a cigarette. He accepted, though still eyeing me somewhat suspiciously as I opened my case. The dog continued to growl. I said I hoped it wouldn't attack me again. He kicked at it and it slunk off into the undergrowth, settling in the grass, its head between its paws, a hurt expression on its face.

The sight of the provisions in my case excited the shepherd. Vodka, he hadn't tasted it in years. Reluctantly I let him take a mouthful.

'Why do you carry all these supplies?'

Hastily I thought of an excuse and laughed.

'My mother still treats me like a child. I took her a case of clothes to wash and mend and she sends me back with a caseful of provisions!'

He laughed with me, hastily taking the proffered tobacco and newspaper. He rolled his cigarette in silence. As we sat on the rocks in the eerie glow of his lantern, I asked him why he was out tending his sheep at such a late hour.

'Sheep rustlers. I've lost three sheep this week and can't afford to lose any more. It's my own people who steal the sheep because they're so hungry. They eat the meat and sell the skins in the market. I feel sorry for them but it's my livelihood they're stealing. If I lose one more sheep I'll have to turn to rustling as well.'

I suggested that his sheep were perhaps being attacked by wolves, but he shook his head. Wolves got plenty to eat at that time of year. It was human wolves who caused the problem. I told him about the group of people I'd seen the previous day, with their heavy rucksacks.

'They'll be smugglers,' he said. 'At least they have respect for my property.'

I asked him if he'd reported the thefts to the NKVD or militia. At the mention of their name, he spat in disgust.

'They wouldn't dare enter these mountains, they'd be murdered. Their uniforms are worth a lot of money on the black market because the Arabs pay well. Since people in uniform are respected in this country most of the smuggling is done by bogus NKVD or militiamen. No one ever asks for their passes, they're virtual free agents. I'm surprised you travel alone, by the way. You're in uniform and that puts you at risk.'

I confessed I'd acted hastily and now I wished I'd waited for the train or at least kept to the main road but now it was too late to turn back and I simply had to continue my journey. I said a mental prayer of contrition for telling so many lies.

Finishing his cigarette, he revealed his intention to travel to Karshi the following day. Since there was safety in numbers, perhaps we should travel together.

'I intend to eat and sleep first,' he went on, 'but perhaps you would like to share our tent. I'm sure my family'll make you welcome. Incidentally I know a much shorter route to Karshi which will cut many miles from your journey, although it's very dangerous. Who knows, maybe you'll even be able to start work on time!'

Thanking him for his hospitality, I picked up my case and walking stick and we made our way to his tent, which was about a hundred yards away, nestling in a small clearing. It was fastened down by four strong ropes and piles of stones held the canvas to the ground. Over the top of the tent itself was a tarpaulin covered in black tar, which served as protection against the weather.

The tent was quite spacious inside but the stench was almost unbearable. In the centre of the room was an iron stand, beneath which a small fire burned. The shepherd's wife was curled up asleep alongside the fire and beside her slept a small child. The smell of burning wood, stewed tea and stale urine made my nose curl and my eyes water. I wasn't sure I could stand the stench for long.

The shepherd seemed quite unpreturbed as he hurriedly poured water from a flagon into a battered pan and placed it on the fire. Not wanting to drink out of his utensils, I offered him my enamel cup and some of my precious tea. The dog continued to scratch and whine outside the tent. Muttering under his breath, the shepherd opened the flap to let it come in. As soon as it saw me it began to bark and growl. The woman woke with a start and a look of horror crossed her face when she saw me. She was by her husband's side in seconds.

'No, no, no . . . Gregor!'

He held her to him, quietly soothing her in his own language.

'He's not an official, he's a friend. He's got tobacco. You've not tasted a cigarette in years, have you? I'm sure a smoke will help to calm your nerves.'

I could take a hint, so once again I reached for my tobacco. Once she had a cigarette between her lips, she calmed down, but continued to watch me closely whilst her husband made some tea. The child slept throughout the commotion.

Looking at her, I guessed she was in her early twenties but her primitive life had left its mark. Her teeth were brown and rotting, her skin, though tanned, was heavily pock-marked and she was extremely thin. She was so nervous that she found it difficult to relax even with the help of a cigarette.

Her husband handed me a drink. It was weak and tasteless so I opened my case and took out some sugar.

'Would you like some?' I asked his wife. She didn't even know what it was, not having seen any before, still less tasted it. I put some in her tea. She appreciated it so much that I scooped some of my precious sugar into a piece of newspaper and gave it her. She took it quickly, clutching it to her breast. I looked over the contents of my case; my vodka and *machorka* were too important to give away but I had plenty of salt. I put some of this into another piece of paper and gave it to Gregor, along with a small piece of soap, which was passed on to his wife. I told her she was to use it to wash her child to help keep him healthy. She smiled, smelling the soap. She no longer eyed me with suspicion; I seemed to have become her best friend!

Gregor was now ready to sleep but, before he settled down, he asked if I intended to go to Karshi with him. I said it was too good a chance to miss. I prepared to sleep on the rough ground, my suitcase once again acting as a pillow. Incredibly, the dog approached me and flopped its body next to mine, its head resting on my legs. I closed my eyes and joined the family in a deep sleep.

I awoke to a cold tongue licking my face. Opening my eyes I came face to face with the dog, its stale breath making my empty stomach retch. Gregor was awake and preparing for the journey. I made some strong tea and took out my bread. Three pairs of hungry eyes watched me break the bread. I felt guilty and broke three more pieces, handing them out to Gregor and his family. Gregor and Natalia ate the bread hungrily, while Serge, their son, played with his piece under the watchful eye of his mother before putting it into his mouth. The dog was watching me, head cocked to one side, tail wagging. Quickly sweeping up the crumbs I let him eat them out of the palm of my hand.

It was time to go. Natalia was busy strapping the heavy sheepskins on to Gregor's back.

'I'll be back before morning,' he said abruptly. 'I'll leave the dog as protection. Look after my son!' And, without any words of endearment, he set off in the direction of the path. I followed, suitcase in hand, feeling quite safe with him since the Uzbeks would accept me, thieves would think twice about attacking me and I was unlikely to meet NKVD or militia so high up in the mountains.

Although about ten years older than me, the shepherd was exceedingly strong and agile, skipping over the rocks and jumping the streams like a mountain goat. He forged ahead, body slightly bent under his heavy load. We climbed higher, leaving the warm sun in the valley, getting up into the snow-capped mountains where the sun only wet the snow and the cold air of the evening refroze it in a never-ending cycle. There was no path up this mountainside but Gregor clambered over the loose stones, never pausing for breath. The snow was now beginning to thaw a little, dripping off the overhanging rocks. I did not speak, thinking that any sudden noise might produce a rock fall which would knock me into the bottomless chasm that was now covered in a hazy mist.

The shepherd was completely unperturbed. He swung from rock to rock like a dancer, his burden seeming to be no impediment. I followed wearily, clutching my suitcase and stumbling over the protruding rocks. Stopping for me to catch up, Gregor pointed to a narrow ledge, in parts no more than a shoe width wide, which stretched round the mountain. It was the only way open to us.

'This is the dangerous part of the journey, but there's no alternative. Take great care because the rocks are slippery. Don't look down. Trust me, I've travelled this path many times but we need to rest before we go on.'

I looked at the narrow ledge. It was ridiculous even to attempt to pass along it. It seemed to me a total impossibility, suicidal. Gregor saw the worried look on my face.

'I understand how you feel. A lot of people have lost their lives here, including my father. But there's a belief in our country that the spirits of the dead live on and if you're a good man you have nothing to fear, because the spirits will guide you. I've crossed many times and I'm still alive. If you're meant to live, then you'll cross safely.'

I tried to convince myself that I was meant to live!

'I'll go very slowly. Follow me step by step. I can't help you since I have to concentrate myself. This ledge is known as "The Devil's Road" since legend has it that the devil occasionally plucks a person off the ledge when he's hungry.' He laughed. 'Sorry, my friend, I'm upsetting you, here . . .'

He took sand out of his pocket, rubbing the soles of his shoes, and suggested I do the same. Then, sprinkling the sand in front of him, he began his journey. Gripping my suitcase in my left hand, having discarded my makeshift walking stick, I began to follow him, watching his every move, keeping one step behind him and using the same hand-holds. I felt the gritty sand under my feet which helped my soles grip the slippery path. I used every ounce of concentration, blotting out the sheer drop and the sound of the cascading water as it emerged, bubbling, in the chasm below. We reached the corner and, as I edged my way round, I became aware of the path broadening out about ten yards ahead of us. I looked at the shepherd for the first time. Beads of sweat had broken out across his forehead. Reaching the wider path, he collapsed onto the damp grass. Seconds later I joined him. He smiled.

'You've done well! Be grateful you don't have to come back this way tonight and cross the ledge in the dark!'

I was; the very thought of it horrified me. He wiped the beads of sweat with his forearm.

'You must be a good man, the devil didn't get you!'

We deserved a cigarette and, for the next few minutes, we relaxed, enjoying every puff. He told me the ledge was only passable in the late spring and early summer. At any other time the risk of death doubled and to try and cross in the winter was suicidal. We finished our cigarettes in silence before setting off again.

The path was now much wider as it wound its way down the steep mountainside. The noise of the broad river down below grew louder as we approached. As the mist lifted I could see the clear blue water flecked with white foam as it cascaded over the submerged rocks. The current was strong as many tributaries contributed to the fast-flowing treacherous waters. We followed the course of the river for some time, covering about ten miles from the top of the mountain.

Suddenly Gregor announced that it was time to cross over. I scanned the river looking for a crude bridge. He laughed, reading my mind. He pointed down the swirling waters: 'There's your bridge.'

Protruding from the water were four large flat rocks, roughly five feet apart. The water flowed fast between these rocks as it cascaded towards a thirty-foot waterfall in a crazy mixture of white foam. He watched my expression. Offering to take my case since he was used to the crossing, he set off and was across almost before he'd finished speaking, leaving me awe-struck on the bank. With a little irritation, he urged me to follow. I took a deep breath and began to cross, releasing it when I reached the first stone. Each leap was harder and it was with a great sigh of relief that I finally reached dry land, the sound of the churning waters echoing in my ears. I sat on the grass, wanting to rest after this ordeal, but Gregor would have none of it.

After all we had a schedule to keep, we had to climb upwards again. After we reached the top we could rest.

At this point my body protested. My legs ached and I was wet with perspiration. I had to force myself forward. I urged my body to move, convincing myself that it would be well worth the effort, thinking of freedom. I managed to keep going for another hour, at which point I collapsed in a heap, cooling my face in the damp grass, my heart beating rapidly, my body crying out for rest. Another valley spread beneath us, the view magnificent. But how much longer would we have to travel these mountains before we reached the town? Despite the pain, I was glad of Gregor as a guide. Without him I couldn't have found my way.

We sat on the rough boulders. I was relieved that Gregor too was tired. With an effort he unfastened the straps around the sheep-skins and let the weight fall to the ground. I gathered small pieces of wood and lit a fire and went in search of water to make tea. Nearby, water cascaded down the rocks, caused by melting snow on the higher slopes. I made hot, sweet tea and shared my bread and eggs with my 'saviour'.

As soon as we had finished the meal with vodka and a cigarette Gregor wanted to be off. If he didn't return by dawn, his wife would be worried. I helped him strap the skins onto his back and we started to pick our way down the mountain. He was revitalised, moving rapidly yet precisely like a mountain goat, while I stumbled and slid behind him. When the path began to level out, I quickened my pace in order to catch up. I wanted to talk since conversation helped the journey pass more quickly. Falling into step beside him, I asked about his family.

# Chapter Twenty-Two

## *The Shepherd's Story*

Gregor wasn't reluctant to talk about his family. His wife and child were very dear to him. If anything happened to them he thought he would throw himself off the 'Devil's Road'. He was silent for a while, perhaps wondering whether to say more. Then he began to talk about his brother.

'He was younger than me. I taught him everything, how to fish, how to look after the sheep. We were inseparable, but while I was level-headed and quiet, he was impetuous and hot-tempered. His tongue was always getting him into trouble. Every week we would visit Samarkand, taking the pelts to the market and buying provisions for our family. On the return journey, we'd race each other along the mountain paths, occasionally stopping for a swim if the weather was warm.

'One day we were in Samarkand waiting in a queue for our rations – we couldn't afford to buy on the black market – and NKVD and army officers were constantly being ushered to the front of the queue, flashing their identity cards and buying their provisions. We were the common people, we had to wait. Why were there separate rules for officials? Ismail, my brother, began to get angry. Why did we have to wait? His voice became louder and louder and I told him to be quiet, but he wouldn't listen and pushed me aside.

'A crowd gathered round him as he denounced the system. I remember him saying that the officers got twice as much money as us and they could afford to buy on the black market. But we, the poor had to obey the rules, in fact we were programmed to obey the rules by the Soviet system. "They" told us that rationing was the best form of food distribution, but rationing was for the common people. Those bastards in the NKVD and the army could get anything they wanted!

'I was embarrassed and turned away, pretending not to know him, keeping my place in the queue. He was still shouting as I reached the counter. Suddenly, as I turned to speak to the assistant, three armed men in uniform entered the store and seized my little brother, dragging him out of the building into the street. I raced after him, shouting his name. I was just in time to see him being manhandled into the back seat of a car. I stood helplessly in the doorway as our eyes met for the last time. He struggled to get free, imploring me to help him but I could do nothing. The bastards sitting either side of him hit him, twisted his arms behind his back and held his head back by the hair. He was gone and I'd been unable to help him. The pain in my heart was unbearable. I'd gladly have gone in his place, I loved him so much.' The tears welled in his eyes. There was nothing I could say.

'I went home and told my father what had happened. He went berserk, ranting and raving, but eventually I managed to calm him down and we went back to Samarkand. My father talked to the NKVD. They listened patiently while he explained that Ismail was a good, well-educated man who'd never broken the law, his only crime being hot-headedness. But my father made no impression.

'We left those NKVD headquarters totally devastated, with our hatred of the Soviet regime growing with every step. I vowed I'd get my revenge, but my father pleaded with me not to; having lost one son he didn't want to lose another! The months passed and we heard nothing from Ismail. I pray that he's dead for I cannot bear to think of him suffering.'

I nodded in agreement; it was better to die than to suffer the terrible conditions in the camps.

'My father never returned to Samarkand. He found a man in

Karshi who would buy his pelts. He taught me the technique of crossing the "Devil's Road" and between us we would make the journey, bringing back as many provisions as possible each time we went. Last year we had an extremely long winter and the Devil's Road was impassable. My wife was long overdue with child and my father became restless. He wanted to go to Karshi to re-stock our tobacco and tea supplies. The winter was treacherous and I persuaded him to wait, promising to go with him as soon as our baby was born. He seemed to accept this and relaxed.

'For some unknown reason, however, he packed his sheepskins while we slept and started out alone for Karshi. I never saw him again. The following morning I searched for him but the road was dangerous and I had to turn back. The shock to Natalia sent her into labour and I stayed with her until after our baby was born. Finally I managed to get to Karshi, but no one had seen my father. I often think that if we had still been travelling to Samarkand to sell our pelts my father would still be with me.'

The sadness I felt after listening to his story was overwhelming. It was almost incomprehensible that this man still travelled this dangerous route knowing that at any time on his journey he could be killed, leaving his wife and young son to fend for themselves in these lonely mountains.

We continued the journey in silence. As we descended, we passed various tents dotted in the many clearings. The inhabitants eyed my uniform, their rough, sallow faces showing signs of hunger. Gregor advised me to arm myself with my hunting knife since the people would attack if they were hungry. With a bit of luck they'd see he was going to sell his pelts and wouldn't expect him to be carrying food. After passing several groups of Uzbeks standing by the path, we approached a larger group, not peasants this time but travellers. There were seven men and two girls. Gregor's advice was startling!

'Whatever happens, don't touch the girls! They'll try to play up to you, but if you touch them, the men will have reason to attack. At all costs don't show your fear. And don't be afraid to kill them.

They're common thieves who believe they've got a right to your property.'

I walked steadily towards them, Gregor close behind. One of the girls stepped in front of me. I side-stepped, avoiding contact. The men began to close in, one of them brandishing a knife. My cavalry training had taught me to use a sabre and I held my hunting knife in the same fashion. We approached each other, my knife on a level with his throat. His friends gathered round him. They wanted my suitcase and Gregor's sheepskins and I knew that if they suddenly attacked in force we didn't stand a chance. Suddenly I had an inspiration. Feeling in my pocket, I took out the half-empty packet of *machorka*. I held it up, making sure that they recognised the treasure in my hand.

I threw the packet into the undergrowth, using as much force as possible. Immediately they all began attacking one another in their greed to get hold of it. It never seemed to occur to them that there might be enough tobacco in the packet for them to have a cigarette each. We were temporarily forgotten and took the chance to disappear into the wood. We left the path, moving rapidly over the rocks and stones. When we finally reached a clearing we collapsed on the grass, refilling our lungs.

Gregor thought the *machorka* probably saved our lives. However, there was no time to waste since the thieves might be travelling the same road. By now it was only an hour's walk to Karshi; the terrain had levelled out and our biggest problem was over. As we walked by the river, Gregor stopped and pulled his pack off his back.

'When I reach the river,' he said, 'I always say a prayer of thanks to God for protecting me and letting me live another day and I ask for protection on my return journey.'

We each said our separate prayers to our separate Gods, prayers of thanksgiving for a safe deliverance.

The water was shallow at the edges, the sun causing reflections to scurry across the ripples. Feeling the urge to swim, I stripped off my clothes and rushed headlong into the cool water. Submerging myself in the water, I washed the lice from my body. This was sheer ecstasy! I shook the water from my ears and watched Gregor standing on the bank, the water lapping round his knees. I beckoned him to join me but he shook his head. I realised he was thinking of the good times he'd spent with his brother. Eventually I waded back to the shore, my body tingling. I dried myself on my vest and apologised for my frivolous behaviour. We sat and smoked.

Then Gregor suddenly said, 'I haven't asked why you're in the mountains, though it's obvious you're not what you seem. You're not a Russian, that I do know. Since I've opened my heart to you as a friend, won't you tell me who you are and why you're here? Your secrets are safe with me, just as mine are with you, as you promised.'

I trusted this man as my own brother and so I told him my story, or at least the main outline of it. When I'd finished he said he was honoured to be my friend since I was such a determined man. He'd come with me and escape Communism if he could, but his son was too young to make the dangerous journey. Anyway, he and his family were reasonably safe in the mountains, and the army and officialdom kept away – he thought they were secretly afraid of the mountaindwellers. Perhaps in a few years he too would make the journey to Afghanistan and begin a new life there with his wife and son.

We travelled the rest of the journey in silence. We had exhausted our conversation, each one knowing the other's innermost thoughts. As we approached the town he stopped.

'This is where we part, my friend. It'll look strange if we're seen together. I can give you rough directions to Kerki since I've used that road in the past. I'll pray each day for your safe journey.'

He embraced me. I promised to pray for him too, for a safe journey home, and for freedom for him and his family.

It was late afternoon when he set off towards the market place. He didn't look back.

I made my way into the centre of the town, searching for the railway station. I desperately wanted some tea to calm myself down. I thought of Gregor and his family. Though I'd never met Ismail or his father, I felt I knew them intimately. I thought of Natalia, Gregor's wife, waiting for his return. I knew they'd all be included in my prayers. I wiped a tear from my eye.

# Chapter Twenty-Three

## *Karshi to Kerki*

Compared with other Soviet railway stations I'd visited, and I'd visited a few, Karshi was exceptionally primitive. The restaurant was a temporary construction, obviously built to cater for the hundreds of conscripts passing through the station. Bare wooden tables, stained and filthy, stood on rough concrete floors. The smell of curdled milk turned my stomach. I ordered tea, not wanting or daring to sample the food.

Crude pictures of Stalin covered the unpainted walls and a red flag hung over the doorway. The gold embroidered hammer and sickle stared vulgarly back at me. A sign on the counter read: 'No Spitting on the Floor, Use the Spittoon'. The spittoon was half a beer barrel, itself half-filled with sawdust.

There were a lot of Uzbek conscripts seated together, drinking a vile-looking fish-head soup, traditionally dished out on long train journeys to the common people or to prisoners. Every so often, one of the Uzbeks would grimace and spit on the floor. The woman behind the counter would get very angry, waving her hands and pointing to the sign and the crude spittoon. She was wasting her time for evidently no one could read and they simply laughed at her, wondering what all the fuss was about.

Eventually in desperation she brought out an enamel bowl with a covering of sawdust. Placing it on the table she spat in it. It was no good; the conscripts were half-witted and laughingly told her to take the plate away or they'd all spit in it. Raising her hands to her head in despair she disappeared into the kitchen. The conscripts now had a new game – who could spit the farthest and hit the bowl. Most of them missed.

Their game came to an abrupt end with the arrival in the doorway of a young corporal announcing that their train had drawn in. Immediately they stood up and filed out of the café. I noticed their bare feet and wondered how they managed to walk on the rough ground without protection. Perhaps, having been treated like animals, they had almost turned into animals and had adapted most effectively to their environment. This impression was borne out by the toilet, which was a hole about ten feet deep crossed by two narrow planks about ten inches apart. The planks were wet and stank of urine and were obviously slippery and dangerous. All thoughts of relieving myself disappeared as I looked down into the stinking hole. I held my breath and rushed for the fresh air outside.

I still had enough sugar, tea and other provisions but I needed matches and tobacco. Black market trading was not as obvious here in Karshi but eventually I found a man of Persian origin who was willing to sell me *machorka*, though at an exorbitant price. After some bargaining he agreed to throw in a dozen eggs and some brown bread. I still thought it was too much but reluctantly had to pay up.

My plan now was to follow the railway line to Kerki which seemed the safest and quickest way to travel. I was itching to reach the border. My thoughts of freedom had become an obsession and I couldn't rest until I'd regained it.

I walked into the growing darkness of the night, covering about four miles before I decided to rest. Leaving the line, I walked towards a cluster of stones and overhanging rocks that formed a sheltered spot. Gathering leaves, I made myself a soft lair and soon fell asleep. In the morning I decided to risk lighting a fire to boil some water. I was in no hurry since my plan was to travel mainly in the early evening and night when the trains would be less frequent and there would be less chance of being seen.

Hours drifted by. Noises in the valley made me sit up and take note. These were not the usual sounds made by the trains but rather a regular squeaking noise that grew steadily louder. A wagon came into view heading towards Kerki. Three uniformed men stood on it, two operating the propelling bar and one, binoculars firmly fixed to his eyes, scanning the countryside. I moved further behind the rocks until the wagon disappeared from view. Fortunately I'd extinguished my fire and avoided detection. But the incident played on my mind for the rest of the day and I cautioned myself not to be careless. I decided to walk at a little distance from the line, giving myself time to hide in an emergency.

When I set off in the late afternoon I made good progress. The sky was turning red and it promised to be a clear night. Hearing the sound of a train approaching, I took cover in a crude shelter, obviously erected by a shepherd as protection against winter snows. There were sufficient gaps in the walls for me to watch the line without being seen. The train was slowly heading towards Karshi. It was made up of red wagons looking like cattle trucks, with reinforced windows. This sight brought back vivid memories of my own journey to the Lubianka in a similar train. I guessed it was full of prisoners or, possibly, more of the poor young conscripts I'd seen in Karshi. This train reminded me of my vulnerability even though freedom was within reach. Caution was my watchword as I hastened on through the night.

Two more uneventful days and nights passed. By then I was only about five miles from Kerki. I looked and felt a mess – my uniform was untidy and rather dirty, my hair unkempt, my boots worn and scuffed and I badly needed a shave. I looked nothing like a railway inspector. I decided to find a pool deep enough to submerge my body. Stripping off, I waded into the water, scrubbing the lice from my body. But however hard you scrubbed, it was impossible to eradicate every louse and the eggs, sticking to each hair like glue, continued to hatch every day. Ducking beneath the water, I felt the freshness soak into my body. Then I washed my pants, vest and shirt and spread them across some rocks, hoping they'd be dry before nightfall. However, I could do nothing with the uniform since it was too thick to wash.

I settled down to rest but was unable to relax completely, feeling vulnerable in my nakedness. I began to think about the remainder of my journey. I knew that the biggest obstacle en route was the Kerki Bridge. This crossed the Amu-Darya River and was continuously manned. The river itself was constantly patrolled by boats. Only people with special passes were permitted to cross, either by the bridge or by boat. My friend in Tashkent had advised a crossing in the early hours of the morning when the guards were least alert and thinking only of sleep. Once across the bridge I should be a mere fifteen miles from the frontier – and freedom.

My clothes felt fresher as I dressed and prepared myself for Kerki. Approaching the town, I made a detour round the outskirts, not wishing to draw attention to myself. When I saw the dark silhouette of the railway sheds, I said a silent prayer of thanksgiving to God for granting me a safe journey. Composing myself, I headed towards the station, trying to look 'official' in my shabby clothing. Although it was 2.30 in the morning, the crowds of people in the café and on the platforms were quite amazing. This explained why the café had run out of food until morning and all I could buy was a cup of tea. The pictures of Stalin staring down from every wall just increased my determination to get out. I savoured my cigarette, blowing smoke into the air and at least trying to act like an official despite my unprepossessing appearance.

It was time to leave. I had a little time to kill so I headed for the platforms to read the notice boards and to check the incoming trains. The crowds ignored me, each person having his own troubles to contend with. Pictures of Stalin were everywhere, his eyes seeming to mock me as if to say that I wasn't free yet. On each platform stood a huge sign:

THIS IS A FRONTIER TOWN. ANYONE FOUND CROSSING THE BORDER WITHOUT A PASS WILL BE ARRESTED. YOU HAVE BEEN WARNED!

This was boldly printed in red, whilst underneath was a white skull printed on a black background.

At first I was unaware of the man standing behind me and I jumped as he spoke. He asked me for the time of the train to Termez which, as nonchalantly as possible, I pointed out to him on the notice board. He was a militia officer and I could sense he was weighing me up. His eyes lingered on my cigarette. It was almost finished but I handed him the stub and rapidly moved away, leaving him standing by the board.

He was taken aback by this but set off in pursuit. I speeded up and dodged down an alleyway, hiding in a recess between some houses. Realising he had lost me, he decided to turn back. I stayed where I was until I was sure the coast was clear, then set off for the bridge having committed to memory the details of the town map on the station.

# Chapter Twenty-Four

## *The Magic of Freedom*

When I thought about the river crossing, my heart began to pound and my body became tense with apprehension. Someone had told me that smugglers, disguised as soldiers, used small boats to cross the river. Perhaps this was my way across? But how could I tell the difference between the smuggler-soldiers and the numerous genuine soldiers who patrolled the river banks? I couldn't forget the fateful river crossing in Poland when I'd been captured. Having come so far and with freedom beckoning, I had to weigh up every option with the greatest care.

I had a number of choices. I could steal a boat, but where there were boats there were usually people. I could try to swim across but the river was quite deep in parts and probably had strong undercurrents. Or I could cross the bridge on foot. The risks were great whichever option I chose. After much thought I finally decided to put on a bold front and risk a crossing of the bridge. I checked my pocket, feeling reassured when my fingers touched the small white disc.

The darkness hid my scruffy appearance. Finding a good vantage point, I watched the lone corporal yawning in his sentry box. His comrades were either on patrol or snatching forty winks somewhere out of sight. I took out my railway inspector's pass and, with grim determination, began my approach. Suddenly realising he had a visitor, the sentry jumped into action, pointed his revolver at my head and demanded my documents.

As coolly and calmly as I could, I showed him my pass, pointing to my inspector's authority and the official 'Hammer and Sickle' stamped across the document. He was still half asleep, and the hammer and sickle were sacrosanct. I obviously had authority. Without a second glance, he swung the barriers upwards. I thanked him and began to walk nonchalantly across the bridge. The feeling of elation was overwhelming. I wanted to shout and sing! It had been so easy! All the sentry had been interested in was my official document; he'd shown no interest in my name, my appearance or my business. The hammer and sickle had been enough.

Once across the bridge, I veered off the main road, keeping my eyes open for a path that would take me towards the border. My feelings of elation suddenly began to give way to weariness. I had walked and climbed a long way in the past days and I needed a rest if I were to concentrate effectively on the final leg of my journey. A cluster of bushes just off the track offered conceal-ment and I plunged into the middle of them. The greenery formed a cocoon round me and, as I sat in total darkness, I took out my almost empty vodka bottle. I had saved this for a special occasion and this was it. I'd crossed the Amu-Darya River and it had been the easiest crossing I'd ever made! I drank to my impending freedom. I was emotionally exhausted and the warmth of the vodka helped me relax. I fell asleep still clutching the bottle.

The warmth of the midday sun penetrated the bushes. I had slept for almost eight hours! Rubbing the sleep from my eyes, I took stock. I reckoned it was about ten miles to the border. Since my suitcase was by now almost empty it had served its purpose. I transferred the last of the sugar and tobacco to my pockets. I ate my last two eggs, not knowing where my next meal would come from. Leaving the utensils in the case, I went down to the river bank, filled the case with stones and submerged it in the water. This way I'd be able to retrieve it if necessary.

I was so close to freedom that my brain wouldn't function properly. Past events kept flashing through my mind. I vividly recalled the filthy black cellar near the Polish border, my journey to the Lubianka, my years in Pechora Lager, my escape, the bullet that should have ended my life, my Russian saviours Dimitriev and Irena, the interminable, dangerous train journeys and, finally, my Uzbek friend, without whose help I should still have been wandering the mountains.

Now I'd reached the final part of my journey. How would it end? Would it be death or freedom? I knew if I was arrested I'd swallow that small white disc without hesitation, since I knew that death was preferable to life in a Siberian camp. But what if I was successful? Would I ever adjust to life as a free man? Would I ever get used to not being on the run?

I knelt in meditation and prayer, my mind a jumble of confused thoughts. My only salvation was to talk to God:

'Dear God, I place myself entirely in your hands. I, who was to become one of your chosen few, shunned you. Lord, if I had followed my calling, I would not have been subjected to the scourges you have deemed fit to inflict upon me. I am repentant. You have protected me on my long journey. If it is your will for me to regain my freedom, I implore you to protect me in this my final effort. My destiny is in your hands. Amen.'

As I meditated, my mind slowly cleared of all thoughts of the past, leaving me to think more clearly about my future.

Finally I set off on the last lap. I followed the road yet kept myself hidden behind the trees. The early afternoon had become exceptionally warm and humid and large cloud masses were beginning to form in the west. The humidity was exhausting and soon my walking began to get laboured. Although it was still only early evening, darkness began to fall very rapidly as big angry clouds began to eclipse the sun. Thunder rumbled in the distance and flashes of lightning lit up the sky. Every crack of thunder brought the storm nearer, the rumbles reverberating down the valleys. Black clouds now engulfed the mountain peaks.

My better judgement told me to seek shelter before the rains came but I ignored it. The border was so near I had to press on. Perhaps this was the answer to my prayer since the chances of crossing the border in the storm might be higher. By now the thunder was continuous and it was only by good fortune that I heard the sound of horses' hooves. I dived into the undergrowth but didn't have time to conceal myself properly. Seconds later a full battalion of Kazakh cavalry galloped past my hiding place. The officer was urging his men on to reach the barracks before the rain came. I had the feeling that they were so anxious to avoid the storm they'd have ignored me even if I'd stayed on the road in full view.

The storm had whipped up the wind and with the wind came the rain, rain that bounced six inches off the ground, rain that stung my face and hands yet refreshed me after the enervating humidity. I could no longer walk behind the trees; the road was the only firm surface. It took only minutes for my clothes to become saturated and my boots to fill with water as I splashed through the rivulet already covering the road.

The wind grew stronger. Fighting to keep my feet was like battling with an unseen demon. I had never in my life witnessed such a storm. Bolts of lightning fell from the sky, one hitting the ground in front of me, leaving a huge smouldering scorch mark in the wet earth. I began to run like a man possessed, the wind attacking me from all directions, one minute thrusting me forward, the next pushing me back.

Once more I became aware of noises, horses whinnying in frenzied excitement, dogs howling. I slowed down, not sure of my position. Then, as the lightning once more lit up the sky, I saw a red, almost ghostly, barrier and a cluster of buildings. The frontier post! And no more than twenty yards in front of me!

This was it, the last obstacle. I crept as close as I dared, the sound of the dogs' howling growing louder, the horses rearing and crashing in their stalls. Each time the lightning flashed, I built up a picture of my surroundings. There seemed to be one solitary guard at the frontier crossing. He was sitting in a wooden sentry box. The red barrier, the colour I had grown to hate, was down and a storm lantern rocked crazily backwards and forwards outside the box. As

I ventured nearer, I could see that the soldier had a rifle at his side. But he was holding his head in his hands, as if in pain. I couldn't tell whether he was drunk, asleep or just terrified of the violent storm.

Slowly I took my knife from my belt. If I had to kill this man for my freedom I would do it. The noise of the storm and the terrified animals would conceal any sound. 'In the name of the Father and of the Son and of the Holy Ghost, Amen.' I crossed myself. It was now or never. My legs felt like lead weights as I urged them forward, moving nearer and nearer the sentry box. The wind was now behind me, pushing me towards that blood-red barrier. The sound of thunder was like music to my ears, the 'music of freedom'. I was almost there.

I was now in full view of the moaning soldier, whose head was now resting on his desk, his hands clasped over his ears, the creaking lantern sending ghostly images across his body. I was now at the barrier. It took me two seconds to duck under the pole and run. I ran, without looking back, ran with my arms in the air, still clutching my knife tightly in my right hand. I wanted to sing, and shout and dance but the wind took my breath away. Tears streamed down my face. I tasted the salt as they mixed with the rain. I ran open-mouthed to freedom.

I was at least two miles across the border before I finally stopped. The storm was moving away eastwards and the rain had eased slightly. I could hear the sound of running water as the rivulets formed into streams and the streams merged, eventually feeding the Amu-Darya river. But all this seemed distant and remote. I was trying to come to terms with what had happened. I told myself that I had actually crossed the border but I found it hard to believe. After all, the mountains looked the same, even though they were Afghan mountains and not Soviet ones. Gradually the truth began to sink in as exhaustion overcame me. I knelt down to kiss the earth, rubbing my face in the soft mud. Sobbing with relief, I looked up at the sky and let the now gentle rain wash my face.

It was time to rest. Habit made me look for a safe haven. I removed my wet jacket, squeezing out the surplus water, and emptied my saturated boots. Then I sat down under the shelter of some rocks to assess my position. During my quest for freedom I'd never allowed myself to doubt that I would cross the border. At the same time, not wanting to tempt fate, I'd never made any definite plans for when I actually arrived in Afghanistan. I knew that Polish army units were being set up in Persia and Palestine, so my best course of action seemed to be to keep moving south until I was intercepted by the Afghan authorities, when I would tell my story and ask for their help.

I felt safe and content for the first time in years. As I settled down to rest, with the sound of the storm disappearing into the distance, I knew that I had a future. When I awoke from a light sleep, dawn was breaking, a special dawn, the first dawn of my new life. Although my legs still ached and my wet clothes clung to my body, I began to walk down the valley with renewed strength. The sun appeared, bringing with it warmth and vitality, drying my clothes as I travelled that long, lonely, deserted road. At times I had to negotiate obstacles in the way; whole trees had been ripped from the ground during the storm and many lay across the road.

It was mid-morning before I finally came across signs of life. Nestling among the trees was a small village and on its outskirts what appeared to be a military post.

Remembering what had happened to me when I'd been caught with German identity papers in my possession I immediately tore my railway inspector's pass into tiny bits. Then I began to walk through the village, in the direction of the military building. The place seemed deserted. For a moment I felt panic; perhaps Afghanistan had been infiltrated by the Soviets. Perhaps I wasn't free after all!

Finally, I saw a tall man, a huge turban adding to his height, approaching from the direction of the military post. As he came up to me I asked him urgently, in Russian, if I was in Afghanistan. He

186

stared, not understanding the language. I pointed to the ground, repeating the word 'Afghanistan, Afghanistan' over and over again. Suddenly a smile spread across his face. He placed his hands together and bowed, nodding his head as he repeated 'Afghanistan'. My heart leapt, my fears disappeared. Returning his smile and pointing to the military post I followed him.

The sparsely furnished building was cool after the midday sun. I took the chair he indicated as he disappeared into another room. Minutes later another soldier appeared, looking at me with apprehension before himself disappearing into the same room. I remained seated, sweat making my palms sticky as I clasped and unclasped my hands. Then another soldier appeared from nowhere, with a rifle slung loosely over his shoulder. He escorted me into the other room.

Sitting behind a desk were the two soldiers I'd already met. They took out their identity papers, pointed to them and then pointed to me. I shook my head. Still speaking in Russian I told them I was Polish, that I had escaped from Russia and that I was in desperate need of their help. They didn't understand a word. I turned to Polish but still they didn't understand. In desperation I spoke in German and this time they seemed to grasp that I was Polish.

Telephone calls were made. Not understanding the language, I sat tensely on the edge of my chair, awaiting the outcome. The soldiers smiled at me and, wanting to show that I too was friendly, I returned their smiles. Eventually they stood up and beckoned me to follow. I had no idea where they were taking me but my fate was in their hands.

As we left the building we made for a waiting jeep. For one awful moment, I panicked at the thought that they were taking me back to the Soviet border. What a relief when the driver set off south, deeper into Afghanistan. We travelled over very rough terrain for about half an hour, with the jeep bouncing up and down over deep ruts, until we reached what was obviously a headquarters building. I was ushered into a large room with my escorts. There was a huge map pinned to the wall and I eagerly retraced my journey for them. They seemed to accept that I was a Pole and that I had escaped from Siberia.

They mimed 'food and drink' and I accepted eagerly. Bread, eggs and a cup of strong coffee were brought and I ate hungrily. I took out my *machorka* and offered it around but to our disappointment it refused to light owing to the soaking it had received during the storm.

We were interrupted by the arrival of a distinguished-looking, smartly-dressed man. He wore a long Afghan tunic belted at the waist and long baggy trousers tied at the ankles. On his head was a black sheepskin hat and a pair of old-fashioned glasses were balanced on the edge of his nose. Seeing our plight, he immediately went to his desk and took out a full packet of cigarettes which he handed round. I took one and inhaled. The luxury of it! I couldn't remember ever receiving such preferential treatment.

We drank coffee and smoked cigarettes. I found he was an interpreter and spoke fluent Russian. I told him how I'd been caught in the storm. To give veracity to my story, I showed him my swollen legs and bitten body. He caught sight of my knife but made no attempt to have it confiscated. I felt safe and relaxed, so different from my previous brushes with authority. Casually he started to ask me questions. What was my nationality? I told him Polish. He asked me to speak in Polish, which I did, as well as in German and Russian, my other main languages. He answered me accordingly since he too was fluent in all three. He asked me my name, age, why I'd been sent to the labour camp, how I'd escaped. I told him my story, showing him my scarred neck, choking back tears of emotion as I described the kindness done to me on my route south. I talked for two hours, drinking endless cups of coffee and smoking countless cigarettes. The interpreter studied the map trying to put my journey into perspective.

'You are a very lucky man,' he said at last. 'Many try to flee from the Soviet regime but few are successful. The frontier is guarded by vicious dogs and the sentries don't ask questions; they shoot first and feed the corpses to the hungry pack. We've seen this with our own eyes but we can't help for fear of the dogs being set upon us. The storm was your saviour. Had it been a clear night, we wouldn't have been holding this conversation.'

He turned and looked at me directly.

'What are your plans now you're a free man?'

I said I wanted to join a Polish army unit, possibly in Persia or Palestine, where I'd heard they were being formed. My aim was to fight for my country against the Germans and, if necessary, against the Russians. He seemed sympathetic and offered to help, but meanwhile I must earn my keep by doing light work in the army kitchen. I needed to eat well to build up my strength; I was just skin and bones. With that he shook hands and embraced me, wishing me luck and a safe journey when I finally travelled to join my countrymen.

My escorts then took me for a bath. With the help of a bar of soap and a soft scrubbing brush I cleaned my body from head to toe, shaving off my thick knotted beard and cutting my hair as short as possible to get rid of the lice. I'd been given an Afghan uniform and felt quite impressed with my new image as I took my old railway uniform into the yard and burned it. I was eager to start my new life.

Regimentation in the Afghan army was non-existent and the kitchen work was easy. I spent much of my time eating along with the young soldiers who were doing their compulsory stint of kitchen duties. The language barrier proved a problem at first but I'd always excelled at languages and it didn't take me long to pick up some basic vocabulary which, with the aid of sign language, helped me to communicate. For two months I worked in the kitchens.

Eventually, just as I was beginning to get impatient, I was summoned to headquarters where the interpreter was waiting for me with the good news: I was to rejoin the Polish army. I was taken to Pahlevi, on the Caspian Sea, and from there I went to Palestine, where I came under the protection of the British. As a result I eventually found myself on British soil. In Britain I was trained as a paratrooper to keep contact with the Polish Underground Army, known as the *Armia Krajowa* or AK.

At last I was fighting for the freedom of my fatherland.

# *Postscript*

I never forgot my family and I tried all I knew to make contact with them. In Britain I approached the Red Cross for help. Eventually, after a long delay, I received news that my father, with the help of my brother who'd been forced to serve in the Soviet army, had returned to Poland from Siberia where he'd spent many years. As a result, his health had deteriorated and he died shortly after his return. My mother was lost forever in the labour camps and died, along with millions of others, of frostbite and starvation. She was buried in a shallow grave, another innocent victim of the Communist regime.

As for me, after the war I knew that Poland wouldn't be free and I couldn't contemplate becoming a slave to the Communists yet again.

I had suffered too much to obtain my freedom. I decided to stay in England. I met and married a wonderful English girl and applied for British nationality. We have three grown-up children who have helped and encouraged me to write this book. We also have three grandsons and a granddaughter, who I hope and believe will always have their freedom.

We live in a peaceful village. As I compare our present lives with the total and hopeless misery of the labour camps and think of the millions who died there I, like countless others, ask myself why. Was it all to pin another medal on some colonel's breast? To reach another target and to exceed another norm? To satisfy sadistic urges? To consolidate Communist rule at home in preparation for world conquest? Who knows? The recent collapse of Communism renders even more pointless and obscene the mass slaughter of innocent lives. Freedom was my guiding star and I rejoice that in recent years so many millions have achieved it both in Eastern Europe and in Russia.

I will remember for the rest of my life the words that I spoke as I kissed the wet, cold earth of Afghanistan all those years ago:

> Freedom, wonderful freedom,
> How precious you are,
> Only those will know who have lost you,
> Millions are dying for you all over the world,
> Only the lucky ones have you and hold you,
> Life without you is empty as a shell,
> And is no better than enduring in hell.